rock climbing
in a weekend

rock climbing
in a weekend

step-by-step: from getting started to developing advanced technique

MALCOLM CREASEY

PHOTOGRAPHY BY RAY WOOD

southwater

This edition is published by Southwater

Southwater is an imprint of Anness Publishing Ltd
Hermes House, 88–89 Blackfriars Road, London SE1 8HA
tel. 020 7401 2077; fax 020 7633 9499
www.southwaterbooks.com; info@anness.com

UK agent: The Manning Partnership Ltd,
6 The Old Dairy, Melcombe Road, Bath BA2 3LR;
tel. 01225 478444; fax 01225 478440;
sales@manning-partnership.co.uk

UK distributor: Grantham Book Services Ltd,
Isaac Newton Way, Alma Park Industrial Estate,
Grantham, Lincs NG31 9SD;
tel. 01476 541080; fax 01476 541061;
orders@gbs.tbs-ltd.co.uk

North American agent/distributor: National Book Network,
4501 Forbes Boulevard, Suite 200, Lanham, MD 20706;
tel. 301 459 3366; fax 301 429 5746; www.nbnbooks.com

Australian agent/distributor: Pan Macmillan Australia,
Level 18, St Martins Tower, 31 Market St, Sydney, NSW 2000;
tel. 1300 135 113; fax 1300 135 103;
customer.service@macmillan.com.au

New Zealand agent/distributor: David Bateman Ltd,
30 Tarndale Grove, Off Bush Road, Albany, Auckland;
tel. (09) 415 7664; fax (09) 415 8892

A CIP catalogue record for this book is available from the British Library.

Publisher Joanna Lorenz
Project Editors Alison Macfarlane and Judith Simons
Text Editor Tom Prentice
Designer Luise Roberts
Photography Ray Wood (outdoor) and Glyn Davies (indoor)

Previously published as *Rock Climbing Essentials*

10 9 8 7 6 5 4 3 2 1

The authors and publisher wish to stress that they
strongly advise the use of a helmet in all climbing
situations. However, some of the photographs in this
book show people climbing without one. Similarly,
some photographs show instances of people a long
way above the ground without a rope and harness.
There are no laws or regulations governing the sport
(except at indoor walls and on instructional courses);
climbing and mountaineering are all about self-
reliance and taking responsibility for your own
decisions and actions.

CONTENTS

INTRODUCTION

Mountains have always fascinated the human race. The Egyptians buried their Pharaohs in stone mountains more than 4,000 years ago, Mount Olympus was home to the Greek gods and the Incas offered human sacrifice among the snow and ice of their high peaks.

We have travelled through and over high mountains for thousands of years and it is hard to believe that some curious people didn't take advantage of good weather to climb to grassy or rocky summits to see what was on the other side.

In more recent times, Paccard and Balmat's ascent of Mont Blanc in 1789 began more than a century of exploration and conquest of the glacier-covered peaks of the European Alps. Exponents of

this period, the likes of Whymper and Mummery, went on to climb high peaks in the Caucasus, the Canadian Rockies and Equador and to attempt Himalayan giants like Nanga Parbat and K2.

Moreover, these men were mountaineers, as skilled on snow and ice as on rock – all-rounders, not specialists. Today's rock climbers are specialists. For them the challenge is a specific climb at a specific grade on a specific piece of rock. There may or may not be a summit involved in the climb, but reaching it is not necessarily the primary motivation.

Climbing rock for the experience rather than the summit is generally regarded as having started in the English Lake District with W.P. Haskett-Smith. In the guidebooks to the big Lakeland cliffs his name appears regularly throughout the 1880s, including his legendary solo ascent of Napes Needle in 1886, claimed by some historians as the start of rock climbing. Leaving the historians to argue about when rock climbing began, there is no doubt that Haskett Smith played a pivotal role in its development, so that by the early 1890s it was firmly established. By the 1930s, rock climbing as a sport had also been taken up in Europe, the United States and other parts of the world.

In the intervening century, technical advances in equipment have helped the world's great rock climbers of every generation turn the impossible into the possible: Cassin, Kirkus, Brown, Robbins, Ament, Allen, Bachar, Guillich, Hill, Moon – the list is endless. One of the biggest changes in recent years has been the development of indoor climbing walls, where climbers can learn and train in relative safety. In turn this has led to growing interest in rock climbing. This book aims to provide the information you need to get started indoors and outside.

Climbing is a multifaceted sport, whether climbing on an indoor wall, on large boulders, small crags or rock walls thousands of feet high. It is also about excitement, challenge, adventure and fun – or simply meeting new friends and climbing to the level you enjoy. I hope you have fun, as I have for the last thirty years.

– Malcolm Creasey

EQUIPMENT AND PREPARATION

Most rock climbing equipment is subject to stringent tests to make sure it is suitable for the job and is designed to be safe. Remember, however, that no safety equipment is foolproof. Treat it with respect – the equipment is only as good as the user, and there is often a thin line between use and abuse. Most safety equipment in climbing is designed to enable one climber in the team to hold another, should he or she fall. Not only must this equipment withstand the considerable force generated without breaking, it must also absorb much of the energy generated as well. For example, a steel hawser would be strong enough for the job and would certainly stop a falling climber, but on arrest the energy would transfer straight to the climber and break his back.

In the European Community it is a legal requirement that all climbing safety equipment is marked with a CE (Communauté Européenne) mark, which certifies that it has passed the required standard of protection, as determined by the UIAA – the worldwide Union of International Alpine Associations.

▼ An adequate rucksack for rock climbing is approximately 35–40 litres in size. Make sure there are adequate pockets in the lid of the sack for keeping small items which would otherwise get lost. Side pockets will also be useful. The other item (right) is a rope bag.

ROPES

Ropes are designed to be strong and stretchy, so that the energy generated in stopping a falling climber is absorbed in the stretch and through a fusing of the internal nylon filaments. A rope that has withstood an above average fall should be thrown away.

A rope will not last for ever. Run it through your hands and visually inspect all the nicks and irregularities as you feel them. Always ensure you protect the rope from excessive wear against the rock, especially when top-roping. Ropes are available in various thicknesses and lengths. Most climbers use ropes 9, 10 and 11 mm in thickness. A length of 50 metres (165 feet) is usually sufficient.

HELMETS

There is no doubt that helmets save lives every year. Loose rock and dropped equipment are all dangers out of your control. In a fall there is also a real chance you will bang your head. All helmets should exceed UIAA and CE safety levels, but some are still stronger or give more protection to front, back and sides than others.

Helmets are also quite heavy, not very comfortable and unfashionable. Ultimately it is up to the individual to choose whether to wear a helmet or not. The best advice is to get into the habit of wearing a helmet from the start. Later, when you feel you have collected sufficient experience to be able to calculate the risks, you may

▲ There are three basic types of helmet on the market: glass reinforced plastic (GRP) helmets, which absorb energy by fracturing, and "plastic" helmets and expanded polystyrene helmets, both of which absorb energy through the shell and via the nylon webbing.

decide not to wear one or at least not all the time. If that is your decision, just remember that rock is inherently unstable, people are clumsy by nature and that most climbing fatalities involve head injuries.

▲ Ropes are often supplied with rope bags. On short climbs this bag can be opened on the ground to protect the rope from mud and grit and prevent anyone stepping on it.

BELAY DEVICES

If two climbers are tied at either end of a 50 metre (165 foot) rope and one falls off 10 metres (33 feet) above the other, then the only way his companion can slow and stop the fall is to prevent the slack rope from running out. But the energy generated by the fall and the small diameter of the rope make this impossible with the hands alone, so ways were devised of increasing the friction on the rope attached to the person climbing, to make the slack rope controllable.

Introduced in the early 1970s, belay devices use a simple jamming system to dramatically increase the friction,

making the running rope easier to control and stop in the event of a fall. A range of different devices offering various levels of friction are available.

▲ A belay device in use.

WIRES, SLINGS AND CAMS

Wires, camming devices (or cams), slings and quickdraws are the essential items of safety equipment used to secure one climber to the rock so that he can hold the leader's rope while he climbs. This is the essence of modern rock climbing. The person holding the rope is called the belayer, he is attached to the rock with belay anchors, the action he performs is belaying and he uses a belay device.

Wires, camming devices, slings and quickdraws can also be used by the lead climber to protect the rope as he climbs, reducing the distance travelled should he fall.

▼ Aluminium snaplinks, or karabiners, are used to attach wires, camming devices and quickdraws to a bandoleer for easy carrying. Also illustrated is a karabiner with a locking screwgate and slings. Collectively, this equipment is known as "the rack".

◄ Wires are aluminium wedges on a swaged loop of wire. The wedge is jammed in a crack in the rock and clipped via a quickdraw to the rope when leading or tied to the rope as a secure anchor for belaying.

Karabiners – the vital link

Putting a sling over a spike of rock or placing a wire or camming device in a crack is one thing, but how do you attach it to the rope? Karabiners provide the answer, allowing quick attachment and disengagement of the climbing rope.

Made from strong, lightweight aluminium alloy, these snaplinks have a sprung gate on one side and are similar to devices used in many other sports. The gate is easily opened to receive or remove whatever the karabiner is being clipped to, but will always spring shut. Not only does this ensure whatever has been clipped in doesn't come out, it also ensures that the gate preserves the "oval" strength of the karabiner in a fall. Closed karabiners can withstand substantial loadings.

Screwgate karabiners have a threaded sleeve which can be screwed over the gate to prevent it opening. There should be two or three screwgate karabiners on the rack to use with belay anchors.

▲ Like a wire, a mechanical camming device can also be placed in a crack and clipped via a quickdraw to the rope when leading, or tied to the rope as a secure anchor for belaying.

▼ Quickdraws are tape loops with a karabiner at both ends. One karabiner can be attached to a wire, camming device, bolt or piton and the other to the climbing rope.

HARNESSES

A wide variety of harnesses is available from a range of manufacturers worldwide. Some are pared down to very little for Alpine and Himalayan mountaineering; some are well padded for the frequent falls experienced in some types of climbing; and some have adjustable leg loops, excellent for those with larger than average thighs.

All consist of a waist belt and leg loops. Some harnesses combine waist belt and leg loops as a single unit while others allow you to mix different sizes of waist belt and non-adjustable leg loops to suit your personal dimensions.

It is important when buying a harness to read the manufacturer's instructions carefully and follow them at all times. Throughout the book, you will see many instances of correct and incorrect use.

► This is a simple harness designed for beginners. The harness waist belt cannot be undone completely and consequently a "step-in" system has to be employed when putting it on. The harness is foolproof provided it is not accidentally twisted when pulled on.

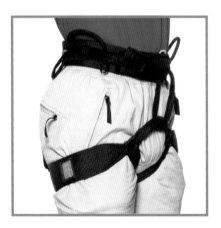

▲ This is a particularly comfortable harness, since it has been tailored to the contours of the body. There is extra padding where needed and plentiful equipment-carrying loops for those longer routes. Although still a simple design, this is a harness for those who are committed to rock climbing.

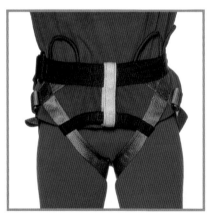

▲ This harness is perhaps more suitable for general mountaineering, although it still works extremely well as a basic harness. There is less padding, but the harness is more adjustable. It is important with this type of harness not to tighten the leg loops too much as this will pull the waist belt down and position it over the hips rather than safely around the waist.

▲ This harness offers the best combination with good padding, adjustability and plentiful equipment loops. All the harnesses shown here have an integral load-bearing loop at the front, often called the belay loop. However, it should be called the abseil (rappel) loop and will be referred to as either this or the main load-bearing loop throughout the text.

CLOTHING

Clothing is very much a personal choice, but loose-fitting, stretchy garments are best, allowing freedom of movement and warmth when outdoors. T-shirts and shorts will suit most indoor activities, although longer, lightweight, stretchy sports leggings will offer more protection for the knees. Lightweight or midweight fleece tops and sweatshirts are good indoors and on fine days outside. Tracksuit bottoms are a cheap compromise both for indoors and out, but you may need an additional layer underneath on chilly days outside.

◀ A fleece top will be essential both indoors and out, providing a good insulation layer. Modern outdoor clothing works best if several layers are worn so you can shed or add clothing to suit a range of temperatures, as necessary.

▶ Loose-fitting but functional sweatshirts and cycle shorts allow the freedom of movement necessary for climbing and are suitable for indoors and warmer weather outdoors.

◀ This lightweight jacket offers both a wind and showerproof layer when worn over a fleece top. It also packs up very small when not needed.

▶ A zipped jacket will give more ventilation on warmer days. The close-fitting bottoms are excellent, offering freedom of movement and warmth even on cool days.

For a rainy day...

Although climbing in the rain is not recommended, some hardy souls do it, and a set of wind and waterproof clothing is essential. Many fully waterproof mountain jackets are made from fabrics with a special waterproof membrane between the two outer layers. Others are made of polyurethane coated fabrics or from fabric which has been treated in other ways so it can be re-proofed. The disadvantage of some waterproof jackets is that they cause a build-up of condensation on the inside, due to body heat. The more advanced fabrics are breathable, allowing the condensation to pass through the membrane into the outer shell.

ROCK BOOTS AND OTHER ESSENTIALS

▲ Chalk is used to improve finger grip and to mop up perspiration on the hands when climbing. It is available either in a block form, which will crumble easily in the fingers, or in cloth balls, which will only allow a small amount on to the fingers. Most indoor walls will allow only certain types of chalk to be used, so check first.

▶ Maps and guidebooks pinpoint climbing areas and also depict the actual routes on each crag. Some guidebooks feature simple line drawings of each climb, annotated with easily understood symbols highlighting particular difficulties, protection and where to belay, for example. Others are more traditional, with descriptive text and either photographs or diagrams.

▶ Always carry a whistle for summoning help in the event of an accident, and a small first-aid kit for dealing with minor cuts and bruises.

▼ A pair of fleece gloves is essential on cold days. The ones shown here have leather palms and fingers for improving grip on the rope.

◀ Rock boots (left) are light, flexible and thin soled to allow the climber to feel the footholds. The smooth rubber sole maximizes friction on dry rock, but means the boots do not perform well on wet grass and they can be uncomfortable for walking in. Different rock boots suit different styles and abilities of climbing and most will stretch when worn. Walking boots and approach shoes (right) are designed to protect the foot and absorb impact. The sole has a pronounced tread capable of giving traction on all terrain. Climbing in boots is perfectly acceptable, if clumsy.

PREPARATION

Any sport requires preparation, sometimes mental but in the case of climbing mostly physical. We call this warming up and it is particularly important in climbing in order to avoid injuries. Cold muscles and tendons are easily stretched and damaged because they are cold and stiff. Walking to a mountain crag in the heat of a summer's day is far removed from the realities of walking from the car park to the local indoor wall on a cool autumnal evening. Nevertheless, even on a summer's day, it is still worthwhile doing a few gentle exercises.

The walk up to the crag will warm your cardiovascular system and get the blood circulating nicely, but remember to stretch the major muscle groups of the legs, arms and back first to help avoid injuries, particularly if your intended route has a difficult start. It will take only a couple of minutes and will save problems later in the day.

There are two ways of warming up for indoor walls. One is to do some easy low level climbing – or bouldering – for a few minutes. There is usually a small area of wall available for this. Make sure it is easy – nothing too stretchy or dynamic – just gently limbering up on big holds near to the ground. Take your time and make absolutely sure that you are thoroughly warmed up before you attempt anything which puts a severe strain on fingers or tendons. These parts of the body, along with the elbow and shoulder joints, are particularly susceptible to injuries in rock climbing.

The other way of warming up is to do a series of exercises starting with jogging or running on the spot. This has

▲ Two warm-up methods are shown here. The climber at the back of the picture has chosen to do some easy bouldering, while the other is running on the spot.

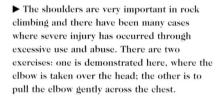

▶ The shoulders are very important in rock climbing and there have been many cases where severe injury has occurred through excessive use and abuse. There are two exercises: one is demonstrated here, where the elbow is taken over the head; the other is to pull the elbow gently across the chest.

▲ A very important warm-up procedure is to stretch the hamstrings, which run down the back of the thigh and buttock. Sit somewhere comfortable away from the wall. Bend one leg so that it lies flat on the floor and tuck the foot up close to your body; stretch the other leg out in front of you. Take your head down towards the outstretched leg and hold for six seconds. Repeat with the other leg.

the same effect as walking to a crag and simply gets the blood flowing through the major muscles. After that go through each of the exercises shown, beginning with the hamstrings. Start gently, and gradually increase the amount of stretch. Remember to always warm up before starting any stretching exercises, and only hold each stretch for a maximum of six seconds. Follow the same routine each time you go climbing.

▲ This is an ideal exercise for stretching the lower leg or calf muscles. Don't be competitive and never "bounce" the muscles – that's the last thing you should do.

▲ This is a gentle form of sideways stretching to increase mobility of the back and stretch the muscles either side of the chest. The spinal column is not designed to move a great deal so don't force it.

▲ The thigh muscles, or quads, are the largest muscles in the body. To stretch these simply lean against a wall for support and pull each leg back with the hand as far as you can. Don't force the knee joint any further than is comfortable.

Doing it wrong

This is a rotating exercise for the back and, as demonstrated here, a telling example of taking things too far. Any exercise like this should not involve either the knees or the pelvis; these are two parts of the body that should not be subject to any twisting whatsoever. Any rotating of the spine should start from the pelvis upwards and not include the whole body.

Warming down

Finally, what is also important is to warm down again after climbing. This will help disperse lactic acids that build up in the muscles during strenuous exercise. Follow the same procedure as for warming up.

UNDERSTANDING CLIMBING

Although rock climbing is an active sport, you don't have to be particularly fit to participate. True, you will need some agility and suppleness but almost anyone can have a go. The advent of indoor walls has brought the sport within easy reach of many who would never have even dreamt of rock climbing. The thing to remember is that it's not the standard at which you climb that matters: it's a sport where you can find your own level and enjoy the physical challenge and exercise it presents.

Rock climbing comprises many different activities within the overall sport. There's top-roping and leading indoors and outdoors, and bouldering indoors and outdoors. Leading outdoors can be on traditional climbs or on sports climbs with fixed protection. These climbs can be a single rope length, or pitch, or multipitch. The following pages are just an introduction to the different types of climbing, which are then described in more detail later.

TOP-ROPING INDOORS

Top-roping is how most people begin climbing on climbing walls. The rope and the top anchor are usually in place on the wall. The climber first ties the rope into his harness. As he ascends the belayer takes in the rope through a belay device. At the top, the belayer lets the rope out slowly and the climber descends. The climbers then swap roles.

◄ This is a good example of top-roping indoors where the rope is taken from the climber's harness, up through a top anchor and then to the belayer.

LEADING INDOORS

After top-roping most climbers progress to leading. Here the belayer pays the rope out through a belay device as the climber ascends. Quickdraws are usually in place at regular intervals, with one karabiner clipped to the eye bolts built into the fabric of the wall. The leader first ties the rope into his harness, then, as he climbs he clips the rope on to the quickdraw's other karabiner thereby creating a "top-rope" scenario should be fall. In this way, he protects himself to the top of the climb from where the belayer can gently lower him down. The climbers then swap roles.

◄ The climber here is leading the route and clipping the rope into the ready-fixed bolts on the wall. The belayer is watching closely and will prevent the climber from falling very far.

TOP-ROPING OUTDOORS

This is exactly the same as top-roping indoors, save for the fact that none of the equipment will be in place at the cliff. A secure belay anchor must be found at the top of the cliff and the rope clipped into a screwgate karabiner. It is important that the rope is not rubbing against the top of the cliff or over a sharp edge as it could be severely abraded and might even break. The climber can be lowered down, or it may be easier to climb to the top, untie the rope, pull in half the rope, throw it over and walk down.

If the climb is too long for both ends of the rope to reach the ground, one climber may have to set up a proper

belay station at the top of the cliff and belay from there. This will allow the full length of the rope to be used to reach the bottom of the cliff.

◄ Here an anchor point at the top of the cliff has been utilized and the climber is being belayed from below.

LEADING/SECONDING OUTDOORS

Leading outdoors on traditional climbs means the leader has to securely place his own protection – wires and camming devices – in cracks and slings on spikes as he climbs and clip them to his rope with a karabiner or quickdraw. This requires practice and skill.

At the top of the climb the leader will arrange secure anchors, attach himself to them and belay the second climber up the climb. The second will remove the protection from the cracks as he climbs.

In outdoor sports climbing the protection is in place in the form of protection bolts; however, the leader will have to clip on his own quickdraws. At the top the leader can either be

lowered down as at the wall or he can belay on secure anchors and bring up the second.

On multi-pitch climbs the two climbers usually alternate the leading and belaying. Pitch 1: climber A leads, belayed by climber B. Climber A secures himself to the cliff when all the rope has been used. He then belays climber B up to join him. Pitch 2: climber B, belayed by climber A, leads the next pitch in the same way, and so on to the top.

◄ This climber is leading and placing protection as he ascends the crag. The second/belayer is securely anchored at the bottom of the crag.

BOULDERING INDOORS AND OUT

Bouldering is climbing close to the ground, often on boulders or sections of rock where you can practise technique and individual moves. The beauty is that all you need is a pair of rock boots and a chalk bag.

Most indoor climbing walls have small bouldering walls where you can warm up, practise and warm down. There are usually crashmats below so there's no great worry if you fall off, but accidents, usually broken ankles, are still very common.

Outdoors, much more attention should be paid to your landing. Always go out with a friend who can buddy spot for you to make sure you don't hit

your head if you fall off. You should consider wearing a helmet. It is easy to get committed to a move when bouldering indoors and outdoors. This matters less indoors than out, but remember that outside a crucial hold at the top may be wet, mossy, or covered in guano. Have fun, but take care.

◄ Bouldering outdoors is a good way of practising hard moves close to the ground.

THE GRADING SYSTEM

There are several different grading systems used in rock climbing, but they employ similar criteria based on strenuousness and sustained difficulty, length of route, remoteness and seriousness. In Britain, for example, an abbreviated adjectival system is used, grading from Easy to Extremely Severe. Abbreviations include: Very Difficult (V Diff), Mild Severe (M S), Very Severe (V S), Hard Very Severe (H V S). Extremely Severe is sub-divided from E1 to E9. France employs a numerical system, with ratings sub-divided from level 6. The United States use yet another numerical system. The chart (right) shows a selection of grades and how they compare. Also included in the

chart (in brackets) are the equivalent numerical grades used in the British system, which are based only on technical difficulty and don't take any

other factors into consideration. All indoor and outdoor sports venues operate one of these systems and you will soon become familiar with them.

GRADING COMPARISON CHART		
UK	France	USA
V Diff	III	5.4
M S	IV⁻ – IV⁺	5.5
V S (4a/b/c)	V⁻	5.6 – 5.8
H V S (5b/c)	V⁺ (6a⁺)	5.10a/b/c
E1/2 (5c/ba)	6a – 6b⁺	5.10 – 5.11a
E2/5 (6a)	6a+ – 7a⁺	5.10c – 5.12a
E3/6 (6a/b)	6b+ – 7b⁺	5.11a – 5.12c
E4/7 (6b/c)	7a – 8a	5.11c – 5.13d
E5/9 (6c⁺)	7b⁺ – 8b⁺	5.12c – 5.14b

SAFETY INDOORS

There are rules and etiquette in the sport of climbing that are necessary for the protection of life and limb, your own as well as others'. These rules are mostly common sense, really a list of do's and don'ts rather than rules. The most important of these is having an awareness of your responsibility to yourself, to others around you, and the environment.

Most indoor walls have designated areas for bouldering, top-roping and leading, and a clearly displayed set of instructions specific to that particular wall. Indoor walls are often privately owned and consequently anyone wanting to go on the wall may have to sign a disclaimer and have some proof of competence. This will differ from wall to wall, so check out the details before you go.

Finally, watch that any crashmats are in place and there are no gaps likely to catch you out. To sum up: be aware of what's going on around you.

You don't have to start your first climb by leading; you can top-rope, which is perfectly safe provided the person at the other end of the rope is alert, and the rope is positioned correctly and properly attached to your harness.

It is important to communicate with your partner, but keep the climbing calls to a minimum. Indoors you should require nothing more than the words "slack" (I want more rope) or "tight" (I want less rope). When the wall is busy it may be important to add your partner's name to avoid confusion. On the right is a full list of calls and an explanation of what they mean.

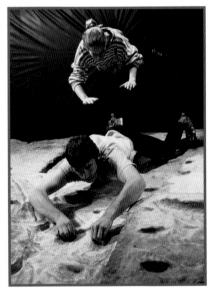

◀ If your climbing partner falls, don't literally catch them but try to stop them hurting themselves by getting close and being in a position to catch their head and shoulders.

▲ Crashmats are often an integral part of the floor but, if not, keep an eye open for any gaps that appear between them. You can almost guarantee that you'll find the gap when you land if there is one. If about to fall off, jump clear if you can. It's much better to jump in control rather than fall out of control.

▲ The first obvious rule is don't go too high, and secondly, help others and they will help you. When bouldering indoors or out, buddy spotting, or being ready to catch someone should they be unfortunate enough to slip off, is a great practical and psychological help to someone trying to complete a difficult move.

Climbing calls

Take in!   I want a tight rope.

Slack!   I want more rope.

On belay!   Leader's call to inform belayer (second) that leader is safe.

Taking in!   Leader's call to second that leader is taking excess rope in.

That's me!   Second's call to leader, rope tight on second.

Climb when ready!   Leader's call to second after putting rope through belay plate.

Climbing!   Second informing leader they are ready to climb.

OK !   Leader's affirmative to second, second starts climbing.

This may all seem a little pedantic for single-pitch venues but it is most important when graduating on to longer multi-pitch climbs.

▶ Not keeping a good lookout… Spot the mistake: the belayer here is neither attentive nor particularly concerned about the amount of spare rope in the system and the climber would probably hit the ground if he fell off.

SAFETY OUTDOORS

Although not strictly to do with safety, it must be stressed that the outdoor natural environment can be very fragile. If we are not careful to ensure we have minimal impact on our environment, we can easily damage it. Follow the Climbers' Code shown opposite and be considerate to landowners, property and others on the crags.

It is very important to climb with a buddy and never go alone. Even with a buddy, you should always leave word where you have gone and when you expect to be back. You will soon realize that operating away from the local wall can be much more pleasant, in spite of the vagaries of the weather. Many people are top-roping now and it's important not to hog the route but to allow others who want to lead to come through. They should have precedence.

Abseiling (rappelling) is a very necessary technique to learn within climbing but not necessarily at the top of your first lead. Learn it in a safe environment when you have more experience and confidence.

Climbing calls are even more important outdoors, especially on busy crags and in windy weather. Stick to the words in the list and use your partner's name to avoid confusion.

Finally, if you're top-roping, ensure that the rope is long enough to reach the top of the crag doubled. Many ropes have a colour change at the mid-point to assist with this and to pinpoint the middle when abseiling (rappelling).

◄ When bouldering, ensure that the landing is good and if it isn't consider finding somewhere that is. Here a flat grassy landing is nature's way of providing a crashmat.

▼ Here, the landing is not good. This steep rocky gully would be unpleasant to fall into, with a distinct possibility of causing injury to the ankle or lower leg.

First aid and rescue

Inevitably, accidents will occur on the crags, so learn the basic essentials of first aid and remember your **ABC**:

Airway

Breathing

Circulation

Six blasts on a whistle or six flashes on a torch, repeated after one minute, should soon summon help or, if you can get to a phone, dial the emergency number.

▲ If you are using a helmet you should ensure it's a good fit. The headband on this helmet has been correctly adjusted to ensure that the helmet fits properly and offers protection to the forehead and face.

▲ This helmet is too high and offers little protection to the forehead. The helmet is either too small or the headband has not been adjusted correctly. The same effect can also be caused in colder weather when some climbers wear a warm hat underneath the helmet.

▲ ▲ Remove watches, jewellery and rings. The last thing you want is an expensive ring or watch ruined or jammed in a crack. This can be not only painful but dangerous.

The Climbers' Code

- A climbing party of two is minimum, and always leave word of where you have gone.

- Take care with all rope work and anchors and put the rope on as soon as necessary.

- Test each hold, wherever possible, before trusting any weight to it.

- Keep the party together at all times.

- Don't let desire overrule judgement; never regret a retreat.

- Don't climb beyond the limit of your ability and knowledge.

- Always carry a first-aid kit, whistle and sufficient food and clothing if you intend climbing on outdoor crags.

- Check the weather forecasts if venturing into the hills.

ROPE WORK FOR INDOORS

In this section the rope work will be kept as simple as possible and, although there are several ways of doing things, the methods described are the simplest and therefore the best. The rope work required for rock climbing can seem daunting but progressive steps should help the beginner to learn what is required, starting with fitting the harness and tying on to the rope, then top-roping and finally leading indoors.

When learning new skills, it is important to understand the principles behind what you are doing rather than just remembering each individual step. Don't try to remember everything at once. Rope work for climbing is all about providing you with the nuts and bolts

of what is required, a tool kit if you like. After that it is up to you to dip into that tool kit and find the tools you require for the job.

Top-rope anchor is a screwgate karabiner, screwed up and facing away from the wall

THE PERFECT POSITIONS: READY TO BE LOWERED

This is where everything has been checked by both climbers and both are alert. The climbers' harnesses are checked and in the right positions so that they're doing the right job in supporting the climbers physically and mentally. The harness supports the climber only if he or she should slip or have difficulty with any moves before reaching the top. Then the harness will take all the weight when the climber is lowered back to the ground. The rope, correctly tied of course, leads from the climber's harness up through the top anchor and back to the belayer. The belayer is attentive and concentrates on what is happening. There should be no need for the belayer to watch his hands. It should be a natural reaction and well practised, even at this early stage. The belayer is close by the base of the wall, with the belay plate into the main loop of the harness and braced in any event of a slip by the climber.

Rope directly above the climber

Belayer close to the wall in a braced position ready to hold a slip

Belay arm away from the wall

Rope clear of belayer's feet

25

FITTING THE HARNESS

There are lots of harnesses on the market, many specifically designed for different styles and difficulties of climbing – on rock, on ice or for use in the high mountains. Having picked the universal or rock-climbing harness that fits and suits you best, it is essential to put it on correctly.

A simple buckle is used to tighten and secure the adjustable waist belt and adjustable leg loops (if chosen) of the majority of harnesses on the market. Fatal accidents have occurred through the waist belt buckle being inadequately secured, the spare from the belt slipping through the buckle and causing the harness to fail.

For this reason, it is essential to pay particular attention to the buckle. Having threaded the waist belt tape through the buckle, it is imperative to thread it back under the first bar of the buckle. It is a regulation that all harnesses be sold with full instructions. Study them and make sure you are familiar with how the buckle should look when fully secure.

▲ Ensure that the waist belt goes around the waist and not over the hips. The buckle system is vitally important: if the strap is not doubled back the harness is not fully secure and might even come undone when you are climbing.

▲ The rear view of the harness shows the support around the legs and back and the position of the back strap. Although the back strap is an integral part of the harness, it is not load-bearing, only helping to keep the leg loops in position.

Doing it wrong

There are three major problems which occur repeatedly when fitting harnesses: not getting the right position around the waist; neglecting to secure the buckle correctly; and introducing a twist in the harness. When getting kitted up, you may be tempted to rush in the enthusiasm to get on to the wall or rock – but care and attention to detail are vitally important.

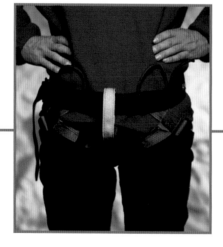

▲ Here the leg loops are too tight, making the harness too low on the body. With a harness positioned over the hips, the centre of gravity is poor and you may turn upside down in the event of a slip. In an extreme case you could fall out of your harness, although this is very rare.

▲ This buckle has not been fully secured and is dangerous. The spare tape on the right must be threaded back under the left-hand bar of the buckle to lie flat against the tape on the left.

TYING ON THE ROPE

Different makes of harness have slightly different places for attaching the rope. Refer to the manufacturer's instructions and follow them implicitly. To tie a figure-of-eight knot, hold the rope about 1 metre (40 inches) from the end, or just over, and drop the end to form a loop. Now twist the loop with your fingers and pick up the end of the rope. Push this end through the loop to form a figure of eight in the rope. The end of the rope goes through the harness and leg loop support and is then rethreaded through the figure of eight.

The rope loop now formed around the harness should be about fist size and the rope end can go on to form a stopper knot (see following page). The rope loop formed around the harness is not only important for the climber but forms the basis of most belaying outdoors, so it should be learnt properly at the beginning.

1 ▶ Ensure that the rope is threaded through the harness exactly as the manufacturer suggests. This will differ slightly between manufacturers but should always follow the same principle.

2 ▼ Push the rope back into the figure of eight and follow the rope back through, taking care not to miss out any loops.

3 ◀ The advantage of this system is that it can be easily seen and checked visually from a distance. Even if tied incorrectly, either with one twist too few or too many, it is still usually fairly secure.

Doing it wrong

The most common mistake when attaching the rope to the harness is to tie it into the tape loop at the front of the harness, or to attach it to this loop with a karabiner. Although both of these methods are reasonably secure, this is not how the harness is designed to spread the forces generated in a fall.

Furthermore, it is better to eliminate any unnecessary links – the karabiner and the belay loop – between you and the rope by tying it directly into the waist belt and leg loops of your harness as illustrated above.

◀ Here the rope is attached to the harness via a screwgate karabiner clipped to the main loop. Although fairly secure this is not recommended. When loaded, as in a fall, the karabiner could open and the rope become detached. An unnecessary link has been added making the attachment indirect and untidy. If the rope is attached to the harness neatly, it is much easier to check and spot any errors.

▲ Here the rope is tied directly into the main loop. This is more secure than using a karabiner, but is not how the harness should be used. Again, an unnecessary link has been added.

THE STOPPER KNOT

As well as the stopper knot tidying up excess rope after tying the figure-of-eight knot, it also forms an integral part of the tying-on procedure and ensures the figure of eight cannot work loose and come undone. When you tie the figure of eight, leave an end of rope about 60 cm (2 feet) long and take this twice around the main rope and back through.

The trick with the stopper knot is to get the rope the right length in the first place, so when the knot is finished there is no long end to get in the way. This is not just for cosmetic reasons. There may be occasions when a long trailing end of rope impedes progress, lying exactly where you don't want it, such as on a vital hold.

1 To tie a stopper knot, take the end of the rope twice around the main rope and back over itself. Then push the end through the two loops and pull it tight away from the knot.

2 Always ensure that the stopper is tied up against the main figure of eight, otherwise it will tend to slide down, allowing the main figure of eight to loosen.

Doing it wrong

It is a common error to misjudge the amount of rope to leave for tying the stopper. If the end is too long it will get in the way; if it is too short, it is not going to be secure. The only way this will affect security is if the figure of eight is allowed to work loose. This is unlikely in an indoor situation because you are only tied on and climbing for short periods at a time. Outdoors, however, you may spend the whole day tied to the rope. Always ask yourself, what happens if...?

▲ The end of rope is too short for a stopper knot so the climber has looped the end through in a half-hitch, which will loosen very quickly. This is a very common mistake seen all too frequently in climbers who simply can't be bothered to untie and start again when they make the mistake of leaving the end too short.

▲ The stopper is tied correctly here but in the wrong place: it should be up against the figure of eight to be effective. Although this will still work to an extent, it will have a tendency to slide down the main rope and create a loop near the figure of eight.

BELAY DEVICES, INDOORS AND OUT

When top-roping, either indoors or outside, the rope from the climber goes up to a secure anchor at the top of the wall or cliff, through a screwgate karabiner and down to the belayer. As the climber ascends, the belayer takes in the slack rope in the system so that the rope to the climber is always snug. Should the climber tire or suddenly slip, the belayer can keep the rope tight and prevent the climber falling to the ground.

However, the forces generated in such a fall are greater than the belayer can possibly hold with just his hands controlling the rope. In the past the belayer would wrap the rope around his back to create more friction. Today climbers use a belay device to create the same friction.

The rope is threaded through the device and the device is then attached with a karabiner to the belayer's harness. If the climber weights the rope, the belayer and the device generate sufficient friction to absorb the force created, hold the climber's weight and stop him falling.

When leading, a belay device works in the same way. As the lead climber ascends, the belayer pays out rope through the belay device. As the leader climbs, he links the rope via karabiners to protection. Indoors this will be fixed bolts. Outdoors the leader will have to place his own in cracks.

If the leader falls nothing will stop him until he is below his last piece of protection, at which point the rope will come tight on the belayer and the belay device. Most belay devices can also be used for abseiling (rappelling).

▲ Similar to the original Sticht belay plate, this device is simple, relatively inexpensive and effective. The friction generated is quite high, so paying out rope may be awkward, but it should be easier to stop rope running through if the climber falls.

▲ This device generates less friction and is designed for quick and easy paying out of the rope. However, it usually requires greater skill and effort to control the rope and stop a falling climber.

▲ This uses a mechanical lever to jam the rope solid in the event of a fall. It is excellent for all top-roping and leading on bolt protection indoors and out. However, the manufacturers do not recommend it for belaying a leader who is placing his own protection. The high forces it generates could cause the protection to come out.

▲ A figure-of-eight abseiling (rappelling) device can be used for top-roping or belaying a leader. However, it is best only used by experienced climbers because the friction generated is very low.

TAKING IN AND PAYING OUT

Whether you are indoors or outdoors, top-roping or belaying a climber who is leading, you will need to master the technique of taking in and paying out rope through a belay device, smoothly and safely. Smooth taking in will allow the top-roped climber to push himself to the limit, safe in the knowledge that he will fall no further than the stretch in the rope. Smooth paying out will allow the leader to clip the rope into the karabiner of the next piece of protection with the minimum of effort and fuss.

The rope between the belay device and the climber is known as the "live" rope. The inactive rope, that which has just been taken in or is about to be paid out, is the "dead" rope. If the climber falls, the belay device will not generate sufficient friction by itself to prevent the dead rope running through and the climber hitting the ground. The belayer needs to generate sufficient friction in the belay device by holding the dead rope firmly in his hand by his side. The belayer should always have one hand on the dead rope, whether taking in or paying out. This requires concentration, practice and coordination.

1 To take in the rope, the rope is pulled down with the live hand and pulled through the plate with the dead hand. This requires a little coordination at first.

2 The dead hand then locks the rope below the plate, positioned by the hip to leave enough space for the other hand to transfer to the dead rope.

Doing it wrong

Here are three careless mistakes often seen on indoor walls. Always belay from the bottom of the wall and keep the elbow away from the wall. Remember, it may have to be brought back sharply in the event of someone slipping off.

▲ The belay device has been left on the equipment-carrying loop on the harness, which will probably rip out in the event of a fall or when lowering. These loops are designed for carrying gear, nothing else.

3 The upper hand now locks the rope as shown, enabling the lower hand to move above it.

4 The lower hand has moved above and the other hand can now move back to the live rope and pull more rope in.

Lowering

To lower someone, first ensure you are supporting their weight with the live rope tight above the belay device and your hand tight on the dead rope below. By slowly relaxing the tension on the dead rope you can then start to lower the climber under control.

▲ The climber is being lowered under control. The belayer is watching closely from a good braced position against the wall with both hands controlling the descent on the dead rope.

▲ The rope is loaded incorrectly in the belay device and this will make it impossible to get the "S" shape of the rope through the plate. It is what is called a "roll-over" and won't create the amount of friction required.

▲ The ropes are being held together so that no friction is being applied by the plate. The rope is going through the belay device and straight out again. A fall will result in rope burns for the belayer.

LEARNING TO LEAD

Spending time top-roping indoors may give you enough confidence to want to lead an indoor climb. In top-roping, you have constant protection from the rope running through a belay anchor above your head. When leading, you have to create this protection for the rope yourself. On indoor walls protection is usually fixed in the form of eye bolts at regular intervals up the wall.

On your harness you will have a number of quickdraws. As the leader climbs the belayer pays out rope through the belay device. When the leader gets to a bolt he clips one karabiner of a quickdraw through its eye and the other karabiner to the rope. If the leader falls before he can clip in the rope nothing can stop him hitting the ground. If he falls after clipping the rope the protection bolt will behave exactly like a top rope. The rope will come tight, the belayer will generate enough friction to stop the force pulling the dead rope through the belay device and the climber will be prevented from falling. The leader clips each bolt to the rope as he ascends, thereby protecting himself to the top.

Bolts will also be found on some climbs outdoors, such as sports climbs. However, on most there is no fixed protection. The lead climber has to place his own protection in the form of wires or mechanical camming devices which can be jammed in cracks and then clipped to the rope via quickdraws. To place this protection well enough for it not to come out when subjected to the force of a fall requires practice and skill.

1 The first lead should be one well within your capabilities. In this way you can concentrate on the technicalities of rope work and do it correctly rather than push yourself too far and risk being unable to clip the protection.

2 Leading requires taking one hand off the wall and taking the rope from your waist to clip the protection. When you do this you will need to warn your belayer (who should be watching you anyway) that you require slack in the rope to reach up and clip it to the quickdraw.

Belaying a leader

Belaying someone who is leading, as opposed to top-roping, can be more difficult to hold because they will be climbing past any protection and will take a fall rather than a slip. Their fall will be twice the distance they are above their last anchor point and this creates a shock loading to the system which you would not get with top-roping.

Doing it wrong

Indoor walls are great places to meet old and new friends but there is a danger in this. Casual belaying is not uncommon and, being social animals, climbers will talk to others as it relieves the strain on the neck from too much looking at their mate climbing. Lounging in a corner or wandering across the room is all very well, but your partner may not thank you for it.

Going to the wall

To lead at the climbing wall you will need your own rope. For top-roping the ropes are usually in place and it is fine to use these. Establish what the procedure is at your wall, as conditions vary. Something else that will vary is the top anchor from which you will lower off. In most cases there will be a screwgate karabiner, which can easily be clipped (and screwed up) before you begin your descent. Other walls may have a system similar to the lower-off points shown in the chapter Setting up a Top Rope. This should present no problem as long as you're prepared – otherwise things may come as a shock, particularly at the top of your first lead.

3 For the belayer, holding a falling leader will be much harder than when top-roping and the force may even lift him off the ground. To avoid this happening, anchor yourself down with a sling and karabiner.

◀ In this situation, the belayers are not only being inattentive while their partners are trying to clip the next piece of gear, but their stance is too casual and could lead to them being easily pulled off their feet if their partners should fall.

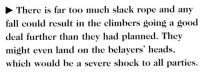

▶ There is far too much slack rope and any fall could result in the climbers going a good deal further than they had planned. They might even land on the belayers' heads, which would be a severe shock to all parties.

ROPE WORK FOR OUTDOORS

Rope work outdoors follows exactly the same principles as indoors; it's just the environment that's changed. The rope is used to safeguard both the leader and his second. The leader, belayed from below by the second, will place protection as he or she climbs and create belays at the top of each pitch or section of the climb, anchoring himself securely before bringing up the second climber.

On "traditional" climbs you have to place protection yourself, using wires, slings and camming devices. If a crag is on a steep hillside you may have to construct a belay at the bottom for security. "Sports" climbs will have the protection fixed in place, making them more

akin to leading on an indoor climbing wall.

Some traditional rope skills have been omitted. Modern rock climbing techniques and equipment have, to a certain extent, rendered these skills obsolete. However, if you venture into the sport of climbing mountains you will need to learn these techniques.

THE PERFECT POSITIONS: BEFORE YOU START

At the start of a climb there is a certain procedure to go through. Having checked out the route details in the guidebook, the time has come to get rope, harness and boots on. Tying on is exactly the same as indoors and a good belay anchor should be selected, especially if there is steep ground below the crag. The leader should rack the protection equipment according to type and size – it's useful to know where everything is before you start. Before climbing, run the rope through your hands and lay it loosely on the ground. The leader should tie on to the end that is on top of the pile. This reduces the risk of unnecessary tangles and allows the rope to run easily through the belay plate and up to the leader. Check each other's harness and figure-of-eight knots. One final thing to do just before starting to climb is to dry your boots. There's nothing worse than having one foot slip off because the sole is wet. Modern rock shoes are wonderful things but useless when wet.

Leader looking for first protection

All screwgate karabiners checked

Both figure-of-eight knots checked

All screwgate karabiners checked

Leader's rack sorted and free of tangles

Belayer facing right way for good visibility of leader

Rope paying easily through belay plate

Good belay anchor at base of climb

ANCHORS AND SLINGS

If the climb you are attempting is above a steep slope or starts above the ground, then the belayer should be secured to a belay anchor. If a fall occurs before the leader has placed any protection nothing will stop him falling past the belayer. If the belayer is not anchored, when the rope comes tight the belayer will be pulled to the ground or down the hillside as well. A belay anchor will prevent this from happening. The belayer can then arrest the leader's fall with the belay device (that is his job), rather than becoming part of the fall.

If the climb starts from flat ground the belayer may feel perfectly safe. However, if the leader falls having placed protection then the force generated by the fall will transfer to the belayer, who may be pulled off the ground and smashed into the rock.

In the first scenario above the belay anchors need to withstand a downward pull (if the leader falls without protection) and an upward pull (if the leader falls with protection) without coming out. In the latter scenario a belay anchor capable of resisting an upward pull is adequate.

The same principles apply for belay anchors at the top of the climb and on long climbs which have to be broken into pitches. At the end of each pitch the leader must attach himself securely to the rock with belay anchors. He can then act as belayer for the second climber ascending the pitch. The second will then attach himself to the belay anchors and act as belayer for the leader on the next pitch. This will continue to the top of the climb.

▲ This is a relatively safe position, although an especially bad leader fall could lift the belayer off the ground.

▲ Here the belayer must be securely anchored at the start of the climb. The belay anchors should be capable of holding an upward and a downward pull.

◄ A good belay anchor that's above the belayer's waist is best and, in most cases, the higher the better. It must be able to take an upward pull without coming out.

► If a high enough belay anchor cannot be found, the belayer should sit down. This is a more stable position and will help the belayer to resist an upward force should the leader fall.

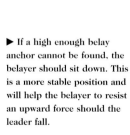

▲ Although this is a small thread it is immensely strong, providing there are no cracks in the surrounding rocks. Test the rock by tapping with a karabiner – if it sounds hollow, treat it with suspicion.

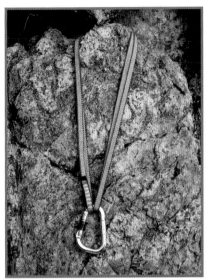

▲ Here a tape sling has been taken through a natural thread and both ends then clipped together. The result is a belay that will take a multi-directional pull and is regarded as the best belay around, provided the surrounding rock is solid.

▲ This is an excellent sling on a high spike. Both the leader and belayer can have absolute confidence in this anchor. However it would lift off with an upward pull.

Poor anchors

The biggest problem with anchors and belays, having decided one is needed, is deciding what is good enough. A poor anchor is sometimes worse than no anchor because you will be relying on something that offers no protection at all. If the anchor isn't in place to start with, you would be forced to find another way around the problem. A tape sling is very thin and easily threaded around constrictions. Because it's so thin, however, a boulder will have to move only a couple of millimetres and out it comes.

◀ This is an example of a poor thread belay. Threads can be excellent as they are designed to take a pull in either direction – upwards or downwards – but in this case the top boulder is simply laying across other rocks and a good heave on the sling will pull it straight out.

WIRES AND ROPED NUTS

Wires and roped nuts, along with slings and camming devices, are the tools of the trade for traditional outdoor rock climbing. On outdoor sports rock climbs they are largely superfluous; all the belay anchors and protection needed are already in place in the form of bolts drilled into the rock. However, in traditional climbing they are used to create a secure belay at the start of the climb, to create secure protection for the leader while climbing and to create a secure belay at the top of the crag, or pitch, so that the second climber can be belayed safely up the climb.

Wires are wedges of aluminium of different sizes on a swaged loop of strong multi-strand wire. Roped nuts are also made of aluminium, but being larger in size they are usually threaded on a loop of rope or tape rather than wire. They can be wedge-shaped or variations on a hexagon. Wires and roped nuts are specially designed to utilize the natural characteristics of rock cracks, where they can be easily and securely wedged.

When leading, wires, roped nuts, camming devices and slings should be placed so that they jam tighter when loaded with the downward force of a falling leader. None of these devices are left in the rock but are removed by the second climber as he ascends to be used on the next pitch or climb.

▲ This is an excellent wire, well placed in a natural constriction in the rock and with a lot of metal-to-rock contact for stability. The placement will allow a good lateral strain to be applied with no fear of the wire failing.

▲ Although this wire is small, the natural constriction in which it is placed makes it absolutely solid, so much so that it will take considerable time to remove it. Remember: if your second can't get it out again, your new hobby could become rather expensive.

Rocks of ages

Chocks, wedges and nuts are basically one and the same thing. You will also hear generic words used for them: protection and runners.

Chocks originate from when climbers would select small stones, jam them in cracks, thread a piece of rope round the back and clip that to the rope with a karabiner. The word comes from chockstone, a large rock jammed across a crack or a large boulder across a gully. The original nuts were exactly that – a nut (as in nut and bolt) with the thread drilled out and a piece of rope looped through and tied. The sides of the nut were wedged in the crack and the loop clipped to the rope with a karabiner. The origin of wedge is obvious. A piece of leader protection is also called a running belay and this is often shortened to runners.

▲ Try to find natural constrictions within the crack in the rock and get the protection to settle with a little downward "snatch". Make sure you are secure when you try this – it might come out.

Two wires

▶ Where a bigger wire is needed and one isn't available, this is the solution. Place two wires in opposition to each other, so that one holds the other in place. This is a technique which should only be attempted when you have considerable experience.

Doing it wrong

Sometimes it may be a case of using placements that are poor but are the best you can get in the circumstances. This is an entirely different situation to using a poor placement for a main belay where there is no excuse. Where a main belay is concerned, always try to use at least two placements. In the pictures to the right it is obvious that the placements are poor and any lateral pull will rip them out.

▲ This placement is poor but in the absence of anything else it may give at least enough psychological support to allow you to relax and make the next move.

▲ This is a really poor wire. It is simply resting on minute crystals, which will shatter if a sudden strain is applied.

CONSTRUCTING ANCHORS

The importance of a secure belay anchor has already been established, but what exactly is a secure belay?

Sometimes there can be a considerable strain on the belayer so it's vitally important to adopt the correct stance. This is always in a direct line between the anchor and the person climbing. The last thing you want is to find yourself pulled forward. Make sure the belay is not too long. Choose where you want to stand, using a clove hitch to attach the rope to the anchor. Keep the rope tight on the anchor at all times.

Where two anchors have to be used, link them together and tie to the central point. Two chocks can be linked by a tape sling which is gathered and tied with an overhand knot. Just form a loop and pass the end through the loop. Note that all belay plates and ropes are tied back into the rope loop – not the harness. This is important to reduce any loading on the belayer.

1 If you anchor to a single point, as in this case, nothing could be easier. Take the rope, create a clove hitch (see step 2), clip it to the karabiner and fasten the gate. All you need to do is work out where to stand.

2 Note the lie of the rope in this clove hitch. Form two identical loops, right over left, right over left, and pass the second loop behind the first. Clip both loops into the karabiner and pull tight. This will lock even when a severe strain is applied.

Doing it wrong

Bolt protection is frequent when leading on indoor walls and you need never get far above one bolt before the next is reached. As a consequence, any falls are relatively easy to control.

In an outdoor situation, protection depends on cracks in the rock and may not be so frequent, so it is possible that longer falls will be encountered and exert a greater force on the belayer. In situations where the belayer is above the climber – at the top of the first pitch, for instance – falls or slips may be very difficult to control because of the force exerted and less energy-absorbing rope in the system. The same is true if the leader falls because the protection fails or is not available in the first place.

▶ It is vital that the belayer is correctly positioned. This is in a direct line between any force likely to occur and the anchor. In a fall this belayer would be pulled around to such an extent that she may let go of the rope and use her arms to protect the head or face. With no one to hold him the leader would hit the ground.

3 If the anchor is out of reach from the point where you want to stand to safeguard the other climber, clip the rope to the anchor and tie the clove hitch to a screwgate karabiner on the rope loop attached to your harness. This allows you to stand exactly where you need to and take up a good stance.

4 The force applied to the belayer is very directional so be careful to take a stance in the appropriate place. This should be in a direct line between your anchor and the climber. Keep the rope to the anchor tight.

5 There are many cases where it's not possible to rely just on one anchor, particularly if the anchor is a chock or wire. The answer is to link all the anchors to a single point and then proceed as before.

Using multi-point anchors

▶ Use clove hitches to lock off on each top karabiner and an overhead knot at the end of the sling to isolate the anchors from each other.

▶▶ Use a simple overhand knot to create the same effect. In this case both anchor points are equally loaded and independently tied off.

CAMMING DEVICES

These mechanical protection devices utilize a spring to open the sides, the cams, of the device inside a crack. In a fall the force is transmitted to the cams which are specially designed to lock tighter against the rock the more force that is applied. A trigger allows the cams to be easily retracted and the camming device removed.

There are various designs on the market and a variety of makes utilizing three or four cams. Camming devices work better in cracks with completely parallel sides, where conventional nuts are not so effective. Some camming devices have solid stems and therefore work extremely well in vertical cracks, but are difficult to use in horizontal cracks. Other devices have a flexible stem, which means they can be placed in either vertical or horizontal cracks with confidence. Try to find a place for the device where the cams are biting about midpoint, which ensures a good locking position.

▲ This is a large camming device perfectly placed in a parallel-sided crack. The cams are operating at about midpoint and any force applied will be straight down the stem.

▲ Any conventional chock would be almost impossible to place here and, although not as good an example as the previous one, this is still an excellent placement for a cam.

Problems with cams

There are several problems with camming devices, usually based on the principle that the more technical the equipment, the more problems there are likely to be. Always extend camming devices with quickdraws. If the rope is clipped directly to any camming device the action of the rope moving backward and forward as the leader climbs will "walk" the device deep into a crack, much to the annoyance of anyone trying to retrieve it.

▲ This cam is almost fully open, with the two outer cams barely working at all. Any lateral movement on the rope would pull the cam out completely.

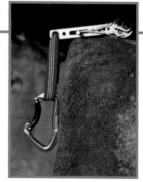

▲ This cam has been placed in a horizontal crack under a small overhang. In this situation, it is important not to have the stem sticking out too far.

▲ This placement is also very poor, with the outer cams barely working.

PROTECTION AND RUNNING BELAYS

The ultimate challenge in rock climbing is leading while placing your own protection. When leading, the question of greatest importance is: just how good will the opportunities be to place protection? Sometimes you can see cracks from below; sometimes the rock looks unprotectable. However, there is usually something there. Climbing on different types of rock, granite, gritstone, limestone etc, will help you to learn where to look for protection. The steeper the route, the safer it is as there is less to hit on the way down. Always get what protection you can, when you can. Remember, though, that the more runners you place, the more drag you'll get on the rope.

▲ An alert belayer on a sports route is of paramount importance, but with bolts at least you have something to aim for. The leader here has a bolt by his waist and is in no danger of hurting himself should he fall, providing of course the belayer holds him.

▲ Good protection on traditional routes relies on the leader getting good wires, cams or slings in position and, as ever, an alert second as belayer.

That sinking feeling

If a leader falls with 3 metres (10 feet) of rope between himself and the belayer, and with no runner, he actually falls 6 metres (20 feet). This is called a Factor 2 fall because the fall is twice the length of the rope out and is extremely difficult to hold. If the same leader falls off at 30 metres (100 feet) with a runner at 27 metres (90 feet), he still falls 6 metres (20 feet), but the force of the fall is only a fraction of Factor 2. The elasticity of a climbing rope absorbs most of the force and the fall would hardly be noticeable to the belayer.

Pitfalls

When leading, if you have a choice between a poor runner and no runner, always place the runner.

▶ Don't have wires clipped directly to the rope. This increases friction and may put a lateral strain on them and lift them out. The amount of friction could also restrict the leader's freedom of movement.

SETTING UP A TOP ROPE

Top-roping has become very popular in the last few years, particularly with groups, where there may be no one within the group prepared to take the responsibility or competent enough to lead. Top-roping is safe, requires less equipment and the few ropes and slings within the group may be best employed setting up two or three ropes so that everyone can have a go. The downside to this is that setting up two or three ropes in one area may monopolize that particular area of crag and discourage others

from attempting the routes. Just as those who do nothing but bouldering should consider other climbers, those who top rope should consider climbers who wish to lead — they should have precedence, although not to the detriment of others!

Two really solid belay anchors directly above the intended climb and a screwgate karabiner just over the top of the crag

Screwgate karabiner has the gate outward and downward, with the middle of the climbing rope clipped in

THE PERFECT POSITIONS: LEARNING THE ROPES

The perfect top rope should be established on a route which is suitable for the whole group. It's no use going to all the trouble of setting up the ropes if only half the group manage to do the climb. One end of the rope should be tied on the climber, and the rope then goes through the top anchor and down to the belayer. This is very similar to an indoor situation, except that the belays at the top will have to be constructed using techniques from the chapter Rope Work for Outdoors. There should be easy access to the top of the crag and remember to warn other climbers if you're throwing ropes down the crag. Upward-pulling ground anchors will also be desirable. Failing this, adopt the procedure used on indoor walls and remember to keep close in to the bottom of the crag.

Clear visibility of the whole route so climbing calls can be kept to a minimum

Good belaying technique throughout

Belay device tied directly to main load-bearing loop in harness, or tied directly to ground

TECHNIQUES OF TOP ANCHORS

The crucial thing with top-roping is that any failure of the top belay anchor could be catastrophic. The climber's full weight is going to test the anchor when he/she is lowered, so it is vital that it is absolutely secure. In situations where there are bolt belays at the top, life becomes much simpler.

Routes that are to be top-roped should be no higher than half the length of the rope. In other words, the rope must go from the climber to the top belay anchor and back to the belayer. If this is not possible for any reason, then you can top-rope by belaying at the top and hanging the full rope down. In this situation there is considerably more strain on the belayer because there is less energy-absorbing rope in the system and there is no top anchor to increase friction and reduce the effort required to hold someone. Always make sure the belayer is in a direct line between the anchor and the climber.

▲ Top-roping with the rope running up to a top belay anchor and down to the belayer.

▲ If the climb is longer than half the length of the rope – for instance, more than 25 metres (80 feet) on a 50 metre (165 foot) rope – then top-rope by hanging a rope down from the top.

Pitfalls

For top-roping many crags have bolts, pitons or specially designed steel spikes driven into the rock at the top. If this gear looks well maintained and fairly new it should be safe. There are occasions, though, where some of this equipment may be old and in a poor state, especially on sea cliffs where the salty atmosphere will have affected the metal. Check it out first.

▶ This piton has been driven so far in that any karabiner placed through the eye will "rock" across the edge and be subject to a severe lateral strain. This is not good for either the piton or the karabiner.

▲ Always pad any sharp edges to stop abrasion on the rope. You can get purpose-made rope protectors or you can improvise with empty plastic bottles that have been thoroughly cleaned.

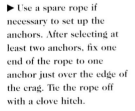

▶ Use a spare rope if necessary to set up the anchors. After selecting at least two anchors, fix one end of the rope to one anchor just over the edge of the crag. Tie the rope off with a clove hitch.

▲ Allow enough rope to tie a figure of eight in the rope going over the edge. Remember that anchors should be equally loaded and independently tied off. Note the screwgate karabiner screwed up and gate out and down away from the rock. Any vibration will tighten rather than undo the gate.

◀ The climbing rope should not be running over the edge – this will cause abrasion of the rope and erosion on the rock. Also the rope is running through a crack which could cause it to jam at an inopportune moment.

▶ One of the anchors is not taking any strain from the top rope. All the weight is on the other anchor. It is vitally important to stick to the principle of equally loading two anchors and tying them off independently. The two anchors are also too far apart, so, rather than sharing the load, they are increasing it.

GROUND ANCHORS

The importance of having a good belay on the ground has been fully explained in the section on Anchors and Slings. However, it is worth introducing a few more techniques to ensure that this important subject is properly covered.

If the anchor is absolutely secure then the ideal situation is to belay direct. If you do this, remember to keep behind the belay device or use an Italian hitch, which can be operated from forward of the anchor just as effectively. If the ground anchor is not 100 per cent trustworthy, add your own body weight to the equation by clipping on to the anchor via a sling and belaying off the main loop of your harness in the usual way.

The Italian (or Munter) hitch is ideal for top-roping, especially if novices are involved. This is because it is less critical where the dead rope is held and it is very easy for a more experienced person to back up the system by just keeping a hand on the dead rope, thus allowing a beginner to learn how to belay without endangering the climber.

▲ If the anchor is not particularly good, clip a sling from the anchor to the main loop on your harness and operate the belay device off your harness in the usual way. By doing this you will at least be combining your weight and the strength of the anchor when belaying.

▲ When ground anchors are absolutely secure it is common practice to belay direct from the anchor. Any of the belay devices can be used for this but do make sure the belay is really solid. However, to protect the environment, the use of trees should be actively discouraged.

Problems

There can be several problems associated with ground anchors. It is vitally important to think about what you're trying to achieve and to remember that no two situations are the same. Look around for the best belay anchors and use them the best you can. If there are no good anchors then belay from the main load-bearing loop on your harness or go elsewhere.

◄ This is not a good anchor. If the climber falls the strain on the rope could lift the sling off the boulder and the belay will fail.

▲ The advantage of belaying direct from the anchor is that the belayer is not tied into the system and if groups of beginners are involved it allows the belayer freedom of movement to help or encourage others.

▶ The other main problem with attaching the belay device to a ground anchor is the difficulty faced by the belayer in actually locking the belay device. In this scenario it will be difficult for the belayer to be able to apply enough friction.

Do unto others...

There is evidence that a growing number of larger groups are visiting the crags, and the rope systems described in this section are used extensively by beginners and groups. It is important not to monopolize any crags you visit. Most of the popular areas are under extreme pressure and large noisy groups can ruin someone else's enjoyment of a peaceful afternoon on the crags. As well as all the technicalities of climbing, tolerance and consideration of others are also important.

The Italian hitch

The alternative way of belaying has already been partly described and involves the use of the Italian hitch. Start by forming the two loops as in a clove hitch then fold the loops together and clip both ropes. Use a large pear-shaped screwgate and not a twistlock. The hitch is fully reversible and ideal for taking in or paying out. The friction on the Italian hitch is increased by taking the dead rope forward and not backward, which makes it ideal for use with ground anchors, which may be below you! Work out a similar system of changing hands following the same principles of taking in on a belay plate.

▲ The Italian hitch is particularly useful for beginners. It is easy to do and requires no specialist belay device.

TOP-ROPING FROM ABOVE

If the climb or pitch is longer than 25 metres (80 feet) the belayer will have to operate from the top of the crag because the rope will not reach from the belayer, up to an anchor and then back down to the climber. Ideally the belayer should be about 1 metre (40 inches) back from the top of the crag so he/she can maintain a visual contact with the climber and yet still give the climber space to exit at the top of the pitch.

By using a spare length of rope (a rigging rope) and tying a knot known as a figure of eight on the bight, the belayer can secure himself to one of the loops while the climber is belayed off the other. The climber is thus belayed "direct" and any slip or fall will be taken on the anchor and not the belayer's waist. To tie this knot, simply tie a normal figure of eight then push the loop back through and over itself.

▶ When belaying from above, choose a good position at the top of the crag where you are in a good stable position and with an excellent view of the climber. Always sit if the anchor point is low.

▼ This is a figure of eight on the bight knot. The belay plate is clipped to one loop and the belayer to the other.

Dual purpose

The belay system shown above works particularly well when novices want to learn abseiling (rappelling) techniques. The techniques for abseiling (rappelling) are covered in greater detail in a later chapter, but it's worth saying here that, in using this system, the abseil (rappel) rope would be tied to one of the figure-of-eight loops while the safety rope is operated off the other. If you do this, the rigging rope should be shortened even further to allow the abseiler (rappeller) an easy take-off point.

Pitfalls

Where two or three anchor points are used always try to create the optimum angle of 60 degrees for greater stability. If the angle of the rope or slings is much wider than this at the bottom point of the belay, the force applied to each anchor will actually increase. If the angle is allowed to go over 120 degrees the force on each anchor may double. If you create an anchor for bottom roping, shorten it for top-roping and then shorten it again for an abseil (rappel), the angle will have changed considerably.

DEALING WITH A FIXED LOWER-OFF

After leading on a sports climb, you may encounter a fixed lower-off bolt anchor at the top of the climb. Before you can be lowered back down a very strict procedure must be followed. Always clip to the lower-off with a quickdraw. The second keeps belaying throughout the entire operation, then lowers the climber to the ground under control. In effect, you are threading the lower-off and can be lowered back down once you've taken the quickdraw off. This is a fairly simple procedure but must be adhered to step by step. Don't take any shortcuts.

It is important to communicate with your belayer, especially just before you take the quickdraw off. Having pulled some slack rope in to thread the lower-off and tie the figure of eight, you must get the belayer to take in again before commencing your descent. By following these steps, you will be able to retrieve all your equipment on the way down and retrieve the rope.

1 Take a loop of rope from your waist and pass this through the lower-off, which should either be one fixed chain of two bolts or two separate bolts.

2 Now tie a figure of eight in the loop of rope and, using a screwgate karabiner, clip this into the main loop of the harness.

3 The original figure of eight tied into the harness can now be untied and taken off completely. Check with your belayer before removing the quickdraw and let your belayer lower you down.

Loops...and oops!

Problems with fixed lower-offs occur when either the procedure is forgotten or a spare quickdraw isn't available. This technique is sometimes required on indoor walls and the first few times you do it can be a little unnerving. Remember that the important part of the procedure is to clip the figure of eight into the belay loop of the harness. If you clip it to the rope loop of the figure-of-eight knot by mistake and then undo the knot on your harness the system will fail. This is the reason why the quickdraw is always used to back up the system.

SLAB CLIMBING

Not all rock climbs are vertical or overhanging. In fact, some of the finest are on relatively easy slabs, where the angle of the rock is 70 degrees or less. Slabs offer an excellent opportunity to adjust your body to movement and balance on real rock. They also refine basic climbing techniques like belaying, which you may have learned on an indoor climbing wall, without the pull of gravity excessively tiring your body or mind.

If you are a relative newcomer to outdoor climbing then make sure your first climbs are with someone you know to be thoroughly experienced in setting up top ropes, placing protection, leading and setting up belay anchors on multi-pitch climbs.

Due to their reasonable angle, many of the great slab climbs were first ascended in the early days of rock climbing. This is an advantage to the relative newcomer. The routes are often well marked and popular, as are the descents. A small downside is that some holds are well polished from the passing of thousands of hands and feet over the decades.

THE PERFECT POSITION: THINKING ON YOUR FEET

We spend most of our lives on our feet rather than hanging by our arms, so slab climbing techniques should come naturally. The perfect position for climbing slabs is upright and away from the rock with your feet supporting your weight. Make a particular effort to maximize contact between the rubber soles of your climbing boots and the rock by keeping your heels down. The closer you are to the rock, the more you will be standing on your toes, the less friction there will be and the more your feet will start to slip. Likewise, if you consistently use handholds above shoulder height, then your arms will tire faster than using handholds level with, or below, your shoulders. By concentrating on how to use your hands and feet to maximize the existing holds and friction, while minimizing the effort required, you will start to develop the physical and mental skills needed to progress to harder climbs.

Head up and looking for the next hold

Left arm out for small balance hold

Right arm pushing weight away from rock

Right knee flexed ready to push up

Back straight and backside sticking out to keep the weight over the feet

Right heel down, maintaining as much friction between the boot sole and the rock as possible

Left heel down, even when standing up

MAINTAINING THE BALANCE

One problem with all rock, but especially with slabs, is that sometimes the holds run out. You can see more beyond but they are a full body length away. In this situation it may be necessary to execute a manoeuvre called a mantelshelf move.

This technique allows you to ascend the rock until you can place your feet on the same holds as you are using for your hands, stand up past the blank section and reach the good holds above. It's a technique that requires concentration, suppleness and balance, so practising it close to the ground on boulders, or small areas of rock with good landings, will pay dividends when you have to use the technique for real.

Starting from a comfortable position, consider the moves needed to get one foot up to the level of your handholds. Your foot may even end up using the same handholds, as in the illustration on the right. With your foot established, you need to shift your weight over it so that you can push down with it and your hands and stand up. As you straighten up, "bounce" your second foot up the rock to maximize friction and move your hands up the rock above for balance. Bring your second foot the remaining distance until it is level with the first and you have converted your handholds to footholds.

1 To perform a mantelshelf move, work out the sequence of moves and get in the right position before you start.

2 Move the feet up the slab a little at a time with the weight coming over the hands. At this point, your hands have gone from a pulling-up to a pushing-down position.

Pitfalls

Some of the common mistakes are shown here and typically occur where someone has tried to get into the mantelshelf too early and consequently stepped too high. This will cause problems with balance and the manoeuvre may fail.

▶ The climber here is stepping too high and laying against the rock. This reduces what can be seen of the foot and also limits vision above, making it difficult to see useful smaller handholds.

Slabs – an Ice Age legacy

Slab climbing can be a precarious pastime and many of the best slabs in the world are renowned for their lack of good anchor points or protection for the leader. Their smooth surfaces are frequently a result of glacial action during the Ice Ages and they provide a wonderful playground for the experienced and serious climber. However, there are other slabs around that are much more suitable for the novice climber, as they are littered with cracks where protection and anchors can be placed with ease. A slab will often provide an opportunity to relax and recover for what may be steeper climbing ahead.

3 This is usually the moment of truth when the lower heel can be inadvertently raised because the mind is concentrating on other things. Step high, but not too high.

4 Raise the other foot and even with few holds for the hands a good balance can be maintained. Keep an eye on the rock to search out even the smallest of holds, which will be just enough to maintain stability.

◀ A common problem occurs when trying to use the knee instead of the foot. This is not only painful and out of balance, but inelegant and in the worst cases very difficult to get out of.

▶ Another mistake is getting the foot too high, which means the body weight is not over it. This not only reduces balance and stability, but also indicates that the climber has not been fully committed to the technique and has not followed the specific stages outlined above. Note that the lower heel is also raised, thereby limiting its hold on the rock.

FEET... AND HANDS

Climbing slabs is all about economy of effort. As a consequence, footholds are far more important than handholds and by carefully selecting the best footholds you can gain the confidence slabs require. In simple terms you can use footholds in two main ways – by smearing or by edging.

Smearing is used when the hold is too small to physically stand on; it may be a series of protruding crystals in the rock, a slight undulation or a tiny edge. Aim to get as much of your rubber boot sole over the hold and use the friction between rubber and rock to keep your foot in place. If you feel your boot slipping on the rock, don't compensate by leaning in, as this will only make matters worse and very quickly. One way

of maximizing friction is to angle the knee away from the rock, allowing the sole of your boot to flex down and increase the contact area.

Edging holds are generally more positive. You are actually supported by the hold you are standing on, however tenuously. Friction will of course also help to keep the edge of your boot on the hold, but will not be the only thing keeping your boot there.

In both techniques it is important to keep the heel down, in smearing to maximize friction and in edging to prevent the toe rolling off the hold.

Rock boots are critical when it comes to these types of hold and some are made stiffer as an edging boot while others are made softer for smearing.

Try a general-purpose boot if you are a newcomer; at this stage most boots will work equally well.

Handholds can be used in different ways: as a hold above, pulling down; for balance; and as a pressure, or downward hold. This is where the fingers, instead of pulling, are splayed out down the rock while the palm of the hand is on the hold to push the weight up. Because the arm is lower than the body and not actually pulling any weight, this uses very little upper-body strength, although at first it may feel a little insecure.

A word of warning: there is a tendency for beginners to lean in and grab a good handhold, trusting it more than their feet. This usually causes the heel to rise and the feet to slip.

▲ The more sole contact, the more friction you will get from the rock when smearing. Be sure to keep the knee as straight as possible. This will have the effect of keeping the heel down.

▲ The foot is on a small but positive edge. It is always better to use the inside edge of the boot when edging so that the weight is directly over the ball of the foot, making the hold much more comfortable.

▲ Here the hands are well placed on small, but good enough holds. The upper hand is holding the climber in balance while the lower hand is supporting the upper body. Most of the weight is still over the feet.

▲ With this pressure hold, the body weight is pushing down on the palm of the hand and supporting the climber. The fingers are pointing down and the thumb is spread to increase the surface area.

FOOT TRAVERSING

Moving sideways, or traversing as climbers call it, is a technique that often causes problems for beginners but again it's just a question of getting into the right position at the start. There are few rock climbs that go straight up and often there will be a series of moves horizontally right or left. The first thing to do is spot where the traverse is and recognize it. In the case of slab climbing, this will probably be a foot traverse and not a hand traverse, so you need to keep the weight over the feet and use the hands for balance.

Plan your moves ahead and lead into them with the trailing foot. In other words, if you are moving right, pass your left leg in front of the right to the next hold on the traverse. By doing this you will have more reach for the next move while maintaining a good effective balance. Keeping the weight over the ball of the foot feels much more comfortable.

▲ To traverse to the right, pass the left leg between the rock and your right leg, pointing the heel in the direction of travel and place the inside edge of the foot on to a hold. Transfer your body weight on to the left foot to maintain balance and bring the right foot through to the next hold.

Don't panic...

Any attempt to climb near the limit of your reach on slabs will only end in you losing your composure, patience and technique and possibly falling off. Always look where you're going. Think and plan ahead. Many climbers retain their composure until the last moves are reached, at which point they rush and spoil the manoeuvre. Keep calm and make sure you finish with style.

Doing it wrong

If you're still not convinced about this traversing technique, try it other ways just to see what it feels like.

▲ The climber is trying to take too big a step to the right and is almost on the limit of stretch. Traversing this way is possible provided you have long legs and can keep a good balance.

▲ The climber is over-reaching, out of balance and likely to get spread-eagled. She is also lying against the rock, which is restricting her view of the next hold. Her left handhold is at full stretch and of limited use.

▲ The climber has brought the left leg through in front of the right but is attempting to use the outside of the boot to make a foothold. This gives little support or reach for the next set of holds.

GETTING STEEPER

When you climb your arm and leg muscles have a lot more work to do than when you are on the ground. Not only do they have to support and raise the weight of your body, they also have to counteract the pull of gravity. It's hardly surprising that any climb that is even close to vertical feels like it is overhanging. The careful use of techniques such as keeping the body closer to the rock when stationary, and keeping the weight over the feet whenever possible, will ease the strain on the arms.

Maintaining composure and patience is as important here as it is in slab climbing, as is minimizing effort by concentrating on maintaining balance and maximizing support from the available foot and handholds.

Many routes have features like cracks, chimneys and overhangs and techniques for tackling them will be dealt with later. This chapter will concentrate on the techniques necessary for rock that may seem overhanging and featureless from below, but is actually off-vertical and covered with holds.

Head turned sideways enabling the eyes to have a lateral vision of handholds above

Low hold for the left hand, which, although not good, is the best available

Good low position with the hands

Hips close in and weight over the feet

Left foot on a good foothold, supporting most of the weight

THE PERFECT POSITION: ON THE WALL

For beginners steeper rock can seem strenuous at first but all that's usually required is a subtle change of position with the body or feet. The major difficulty is not how to achieve this but where. Put your weight on the inside edge of the foot wherever possible. Keep hands and arms low to stop them tiring quickly and the head turned to the intended direction of travel. In this position you can not only rest but will also be in a good position to start the next move. To make progress it is necessary to lean away from the rock for better vision and to make room to use the next holds to the best advantage. This is a fundamental skill required in climbing.

Side pull with the right hand helping to maintain balance

Good wide stance for stability

Right foot edging and turned sideways on to relieve strain on the calf muscles

HANDHOLDS

Handholds become more important as the climbing gets steeper, for obvious reasons. But remember to keep the weight over the feet. Climbers have a name for each particular type of hold. If the hold is large, then it becomes a "jug" in climbers' slang. Large pocket holds are often difficult to see from below and a real bonus on steeper climbs. Sometimes there are small pockets accepting only the first half of the fingers, but a good lip can make them incut and feel really secure.

Sloping holds (slopers), pinch grips, underclings and layaways are holds that require a little more thought and cunning to make the best of them. Used effectively, they can mean the difference between success and failure. Underclings and layaways are described opposite. Pinch grips are used on small ridges of rock where you literally pinch the rock between fingers and thumb to maintain balance.

Because sloping holds are so hard to grip, try crimping the fingers. This can be particularly severe on tendons, so take extra care. However, sloping holds can be of little use when you're attempting a strenuous pull, and many climbers will look for another hold before committing themselves. Use sloping holds as well as you can, and move swiftly. You will also benefit from using chalk to increase grip.

► Pocket holds, possibly big enough for both hands, are holds you dream about – places where you could hang around all day (provided it's not too steep). This particular hold is not large but would give the climber lots of confidence.

► Using a large handhold requires little except remembering where it was when you want to use it as a foothold. "Jugs" are exactly as you would imagine: large and comfortable.

▲ Small ledges often reveal a "lip" and even getting the first finger joint over should suffice. Although the holds here are small, at least they are positive: the body is away from the rock and the feet are pushing on to the footholds.

◀ Here the climber is using a very poor sloping hold for his left hand and is barely able to maintain his position. However, such holds are good enough to let you change position with your feet and progress. Use chalk to improve the grip.

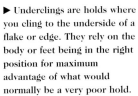

▶ Underclings are holds where you cling to the underside of a flake or edge. They rely on the body or feet being in the right position for maximum advantage of what would normally be a very poor hold.

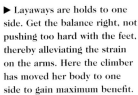

▶ Layaways are holds to one side. Get the balance right, not pushing too hard with the feet, thereby alleviating the strain on the arms. Here the climber has moved her body to one side to gain maximum benefit.

Pulling and pushing

Underclings and layaways are usually very difficult to use until you can get the feet high enough and the body far enough away from the rock to pull on the hands and arms. Both require a sideways pull with the feet pushing in the opposite direction to create a pulling-and-pushing effect. This can be a fairly strenuous position, so work out your next move before committing yourself to the hold. The difficulty with either of these techniques is not so much getting into them as getting out. This usually means taking one hand off a crucial hold to start the next move. If you are not careful you may get out of the move quicker than you had intended, by falling.

HAND AND FOOT TRAVERSING

Hand traverses are where there are handholds but no footholds so most of the body weight is taken on the hands and arms. Essentially, there are two ways to ease the strain on the arms. One way is to work the moves out quickly, the other is to keep the body well away from the rock and smear with the feet. By keeping the weight out you should be able to see any holds and use them to maximum advantage by pushing the feet on to them. That way you will at least prevent a little strain on the arms. Don't try to rush; the calmer and more relaxed you remain, the more you will see. Try to work out the right sequence for maximum benefit from the holds that are there; this may involve crossing the hands, but be careful this doesn't leave you "wrong-handed" for the next move.

Foot traverses are an extension of working on slabs and a very similar technique is used. However, the rock being steeper, the lack of handholds makes things more interesting. Speed is not important because the weight is over the feet. The essence of the move is making sure you get it right and in the right sequence. Getting it wrong with the wrong feet on the wrong hold can be a serious matter, especially with few, if any, handholds. It's possible to get into a can't-go-forward-can't-go-backward situation with the end result (falling off) more a question of when and not if!

All traversing techniques are best learnt in a bouldering situation, where it's possible to experiment in perfect safety. Try being inventive and if it works use it.

1 In a situation where there may be a continuous ledge for the hands but little for the feet, keep your weight away from the rock so you can gain what you can from a series of poor footholds.

2 Reach across to a good handhold and smear with same side foot if there is only a poor hold. Transfer your weight across to a new position. Keep the heel of the leading foot low to ease the strain on calf muscles and increase the friction of the boot on the rock.

3 The crucial thing on a foot traverse is to get the sequence right. Traversing to the right, step through with the left leg and, standing over the inside edge of the boot, point the heel as much as you can to the right. In this way you can reach further.

4 Bring the right leg around the back of the left on to another good foothold. Transfer your weight over to the right. You should be able to maintain a good balanced position throughout the procedure.

WEIGHT IN/WEIGHT OUT

When climbing keep your body away from the rock, look carefully at the foothold and try to determine the best possible way of using it. This way your body weight pushes the feet on to, and not away from, small holds and offers more security. As you move there are three good points of contact for stability and an awareness of where the next foothold is, allowing closer inspection of the rock above and planning of the next move. The weight is close to the rock without being too close, and the hips should be over the feet, so that you can change easily from movement to a position of rest where you can work out the next moves. Getting too close to the rock when climbing is not only uncomfortable, it reduces vision. This is the essence of climbing.

◀ Lean well away from the rock to enable you to see the foothold and make the best use of it. Maintain a good stable position from which to move so you can transfer the weight on to the right leg as you gain height.

Doing it wrong

▶ The climber is too close and unable either to see the footholds or to make the best use of them. This is principally caused by the fact she is reaching too high with the hands. Note also the cramped position of the right arm, which will become tired if the position is maintained for long.

▶▶ As in the mantelshelf move in the previous chapter, don't put a knee on the rock. It's painful, makes it awkward to maintain balance, and it is very easy to get into a can't-go-up-can't-go-down situation.

RESTING TIRED ARMS

Any situation where your arms are above the head will quickly tire them and make frequent resting necessary.

Straight-arm rests – resting on either one or two arms – is simple enough but not obvious at first. Trying it out on the indoor wall will soon convince you, however.

Turning sideways to the rock is perhaps more difficult to understand. The major difference is that the weight of the hips is more over the footholds, therefore less on the arms. The only answer is to try it and see.

1 Resting on two straight arms is definitely to be preferred, but trying to do so on arms that are cramped and under tension will only result in the arms tiring rapidly.

2 By hanging from one straight arm, it's possible to "shake out" the other and get the blood circulating again.

Doing it wrong

The climber here has moved up and is trying to maintain a strenuous position with both arms locked. There is little or no weight taken on the legs and feet so a great deal of energy is being expended. In trying to see the holds above and work out the next sequence, it is sometimes necessary to move into a strenuous position briefly. The trick is not to hold it for too long and to revert to either a one-arm or two-arm rest.

3 Turning sideways on to the rock enables you to get your body weight over the feet and again create a good resting position. The other advantage is that any handholds out to the side can be used to better effect.

ROCK-OVER (ADVANCED)

A more advanced but useful technique is what climbers call a "rock-over" sequence. In some ways it is similar to the mantelshelf move described in the previous chapter. In this situation, though, it is both more strenuous and more delicate to execute. Used when no other option is available and there are few handholds, except for balance, the rock-over involves placing one foot on to a high foothold and transferring all the weight over on to it.

Even though the rock-over is an advanced technique, it is surprising how often it can be used, even on relatively easy routes. Flexibility of the hip is a great asset, as is the ability to work out moves at least two or three steps ahead.

1 If the hold is high to the left, raise the left leg and tuck it tightly under the backside, using what handholds are available to maintain balance.

2 Lean well to the left. The difficult part is transferring your weight on to the high foothold and standing up.

The "weighting" game

Some of the more advanced techniques required for steep rock involve the same principles as described earlier but require even more subtle weight transference and a basic understanding of mechanics. All these techniques are best practised in a bouldering situation. Try the rock-over on a large hold at first and then progress on to smaller ones. This is another smaller game within the bouldering game, which can be really useful once you've mastered a particular sequence of moves. What you have to do is try to leave one or two of the bigger holds out of the sequence – we call this the elimination game. Trying this with a few friends can be great fun and very competitive. Make sure you are well warmed up before you start.

OVERHANGING ROCK

As we established in the previous chapter, rock that's not quite vertical can feel overhanging when you are climbing on it, so what about overhanging rock that's just that? Guidebooks may refer to such routes as very steep or gently overhanging, and in extreme cases you may find yourself stretched horizontally out under a large overhang or roof.

The crucial factor is not how big the overhang is, but whether it's climbable. There may be a perfect crack running straight across it, in which case it will be challenging and entertaining, but not necessarily too difficult. Or it may be a small overhang or overlap which will require the small incuts and pinch grip techniques discussed in the previous chapter.

THE PERFECT POSITION: SEEING THE WAY AHEAD

In looking for the perfect position there are many variables to consider, not least of which will be the size and difficulty of the overhang. However, the position must be one where you are in control, able to see the moves ahead and able to move on to and over the overhang, as shown here. Keep your feet high, to stop them swinging to the side, and they will take considerable weight off the arms. Keep your body clear of the rock, giving good visibility of any footholds, which will help maintain a steady position and complete the next moves. Once the overhanging section of climbing is started, it is important to keep the momentum but without trying to rush things.

One arm in straight-arm rest

Eyes looking at the next holds

Hand on lip of overhang which is a good "jug"

Knees flexed to maintain balance

Head able to look up and down

Foot on high foothold, ready to push up

Body position clear of the rock pushing weight on to small footholds

Hips turned side-ways to put more weight over feet

Feet using what holds are available

67

UP, ROUND AND OVER

Guidebooks will indicate the difficulty and size of any overhanging section of rock. However, all require a positive approach and the ability to work out a sequence of moves quickly and without panicking. As the overhang is approached, look out for likely handholds and look particularly for small footholds where it is possible to edge. Failing that, it's surprising how effective a smear can be in this situation. Some people prefer overhanging rock, because as climbers they have the technique, the physical and mental approach, and the stamina to rise to the challenge.

All overhangs have holds so with good technique, experience and skill you can use the holds available to their best advantage. If you have to climb down for a rest you'll be glad you remembered where all the small holds were. Climbing down an overhanging section of rock in control is very difficult.

1 Work out the series of moves from below and then try to move swiftly, keeping the body away from the rock.

2 A taller climber could be forced out of balance before reaching the overhang, but the height advantage could give access to the holds above.

Doing it wrong

Many people get their body too close to the rock, thereby cramping their arms and leading them to tire quickly. In this position it is also difficult to see the feet and the footholds properly. So keep the correct position. At the time it feels as though getting close to the rock is the right thing to do, but as soon as you move in and lie across the overhang you will realize your mistake. You'll feel like a stranded fish.

▶ A common problem with overhangs is completing half the move – that is, getting the stomach on the top of the overhang and then having to belly roll to finish the move. This is because the weight has been transferred too quickly in an attempt to reach better holds above.

▲ Don't overreach with your hands. This could restrict movement for the legs and limit your vision for the footholds.

Best of buddies...

Climbing overhanging rock, and especially heel hooking (see below), is quite difficult and it's worth practising the moves while bouldering nearer the ground, first. Always go with a buddy and have them close by you, and wear a helmet. The rocks will be steep and a fall could be extremely dangerous. Make sure that the landing is good, your buddy attentive and that they know what they are trying to do, which is to stop any vulnerable parts of your anatomy, especially your head, from hitting the ground.

3 Don't forget when tackling overhangs to use the resting positions described earlier. Never maintain the cramped-arm position for long and use it only when having a look or reaching for the next hold.

4 Finally, pull over the overhang using a mantelshelf to complete the move.

Heel hooking

Another particularly valuable technique for overhangs is heel hooking, which will take a good deal of weight off the arms and transfer it to the legs. Some rock boots have a specially designed pad which facilitates this.

1 With your hands on top of the overhang and your feet in a good high position, hold your position with one leg and bring the other through. Reach out and hook the heel over the lip of the overhang. The heel hook will take some weight off the arms.

2 At the same time reverse-grip with your hands from a pull hold to a push (pressure hold) and rock over in the way we saw in the last chapter.

CRACKS AND JAMMING

Cracks offer climbers invaluable places into which they can jam a hand or foot to create a secure handhold or foothold – hence the term "jamming". Cracks can vary in width enormously from minute finger cracks to chimneys, which are large enough to admit the whole body. Chimneys are dealt with in detail in the next chapter.

The technique required to deal with smaller cracks depends on their width. You will need to decide whether to use finger, hand or fist jamming

for handholds, and what sort of toe/foot combination you'll need for footholds. Any cracks that don't fit any of these combinations (for example, off-widths which are too wide for jamming and too narrow to admit the whole body) will require other techniques.

THE PERFECT POSITION: FILLING IN THE CRACKS

This is the perfect position, high on a good hand and foot-jamming crack, although the climber is, in fact, only a metre (yard) or so from the ground. The climber here is using jamming for both hand and footholds to give himself as many options as possible. Because this crack is quite steep it requires stamina and confidence. Either the hands are placed in the crack at a point where the crack narrows to ensure a good fit, or the hand is enlarged by pushing the thumb across the palm. This will effectively jam the hand in position and give an excellent hold. Always keep your body well away from the rock, with the hands kept as low as possible in relation to the rest of the body. If your feet are also jammed in this will take most of the weight off your arms, which you can rest, if extended. From this position, you will be able to bring the feet high, get another foot jam and use your legs to push up.

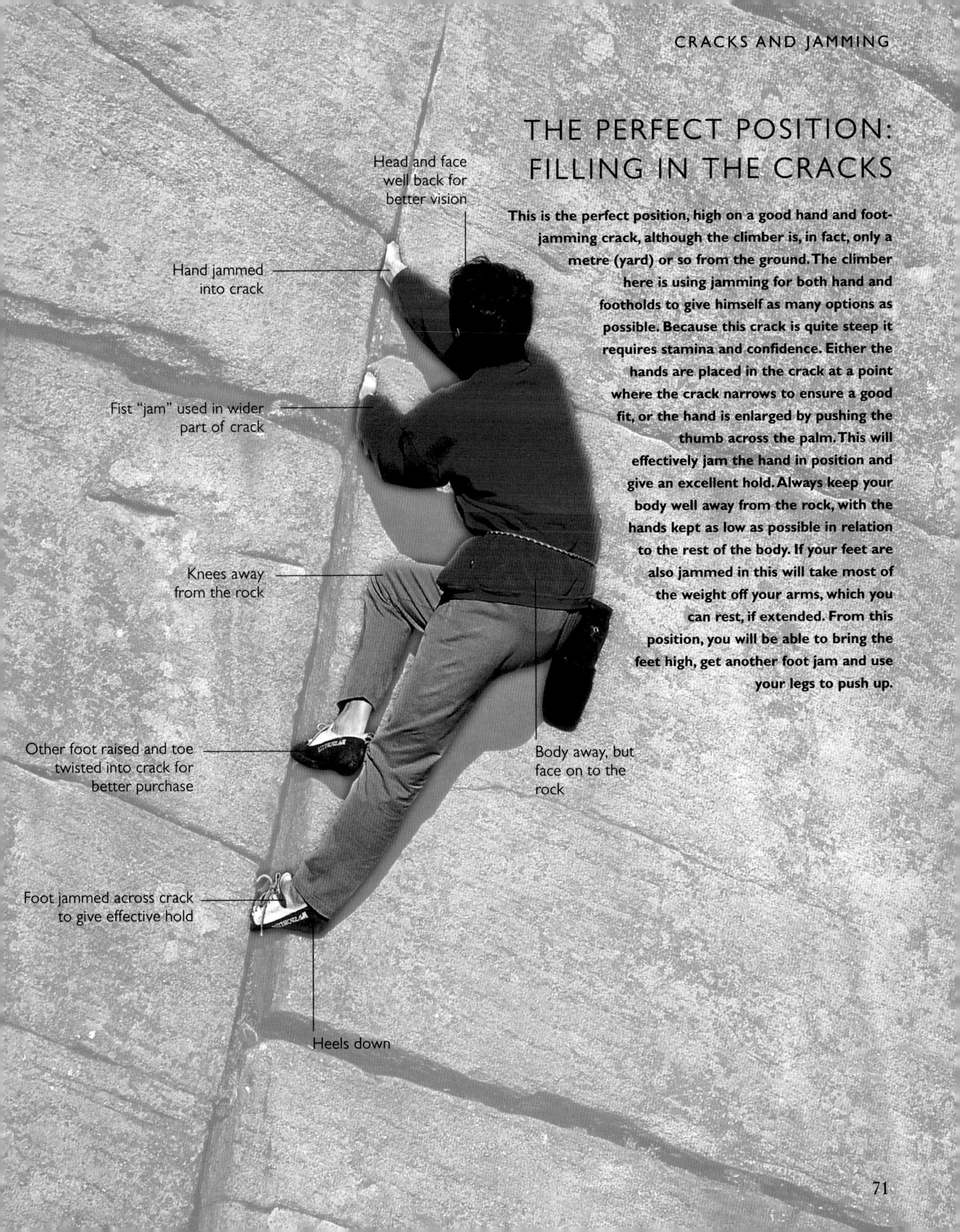

Head and face well back for better vision

Hand jammed into crack

Fist "jam" used in wider part of crack

Knees away from the rock

Other foot raised and toe twisted into crack for better purchase

Foot jammed across crack to give effective hold

Body away, but face on to the rock

Heels down

71

HAND, FIST, FINGER AND FEET JAMS

Cracks will be small but important features encountered within other much larger features on a crag, whether it's a slab, steep-face climb or something rather more difficult, such as a roof. On easier-angled rock, cracks can be a great bonus, as most of the weight is on the feet, so there is little strain on the fingers or arms. They are used simply for balance and extra confidence.

The steepness of the rock and quality of the jam will determine how much weight you can put on them. Finger, hand and fist jams can all be used effectively depending on how wide the crack is. If the crack is wider, push the fingers across on to the other side of the crack away from the back of the hand. Needless to say, all finger and hand jamming can be painful, so some climbers tape their hands, particularly if going on serious multi-pitch routes.

Use natural constrictions in the crack for foot jams. If there are none, roll the knee away from the crack, put the toe or foot in and lever the knee gently back towards the vertical. The boot sole should do the rest. As always, keep the heel down. Finally, with all types of jamming, remember that we are all different sizes. What is an excellent hand jam for one will be the worst fist jam in the world for another.

▲ To make a hand jam, look for places where the crack narrows and put the hand into the crack. If it jams naturally, all well and good; if not, squeeze the thumb across the palm and the hand should enlarge enough for it to become really secure.

▲ Fist jams are exactly what they imply: simply bunch the fist and jam it across the crack. The problem with fist jams is that less of the hand is in contact with rock, so there is often a feeling of insecurity.

Doing it wrong

One common problem when jamming is getting too far into a crack and turning it into a chimney, when the best holds are usually on the edge. This is fighting the crack instead of climbing it and a sure way of getting tired quickly, with the result that you either slide backward or become permanently frightened of cracks. Remember the perfect position and climb with a little style. Don't thrash about in the depths of the crack just because you have both hands buried to the armpit. Remember the little holds and incuts to the side of the crack.

▲ For a finger jam, place the fingers in the crack and lock them on each side of the crack to create an effective hold. For a better grip, look for constrictions within the crack or for a lip on one of the edges of the crack.

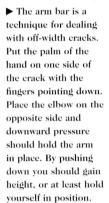

▲ Toe and foot jams are usually less painful than finger and hand jams. To make a good toe or foot jam, look for the natural constrictions within the crack. The detail (above right) shows how the lower foot has to be turned to get greater purchase.

▶ The arm bar is a technique for dealing with off-width cracks. Put the palm of the hand on one side of the crack with the fingers pointing down. Place the elbow on the opposite side and downward pressure should hold the arm in place. By pushing down you should gain height, or at least hold yourself in position.

Double-foot jam

This is another method of dealing with an off-width. The aim is to stack the feet, with one foot across the crack and the other jammed alongside to increase the width – a double-foot jam. The knee is also used to increase the surface area (fleece pants are obligatory) and the arm is used as an arm bar across the crack. Use the other hand to gain what purchase it can on the edge of the crack. The pressure hold is the most useful and least strenuous because the arm is pushing rather than pulling. Always look in the intended direction of travel and at the same time try to keep a lookout behind on the other wall.

All that glitters...

It cannot be emphasized too much that the removal of watches, jewellery and rings in particular is of paramount importance when either jamming or bouldering, in fact in any form of climbing. Rings can inflict severe damage to the hand in certain situations. Finger jamming is not the only technique that might occasion this and it's not enough just to put tape over the rings as many people do – although it's better than nothing. Always practise your jamming technique on easy rocks at first and be especially careful if the first few moves of a climb are steep and slippery.

CHIMNEYS

In rock-climbing terms a chimney is a crack wide enough to admit the whole body. Chimneys vary in width from something just possible to squeeze into to something so wide that the climber can barely reach from one side to the other. Some will be endowed with big comfortable holds which make life easy, while others are polished smooth from other climbers' attentions. Many of the earliest rock climbs ever recorded followed chimneys. In those days the rope offered little more than

psychological support, so climbers were attracted to the chimneys' dark confines where they at least had some security. Flared chimneys, which are narrow at the back and wide at the front, can be very difficult to climb.

THE PERFECT POSITION: USING OPPOSING FORCES

Gaining the perfect position will depend on the size of the chimney and the number of holds available. There are two options – straddling the gap if the chimney is wide or flared, or "back and footing" it if not. Chimneys that are wider or flared may be easier to straddle with one foot and one hand on either wall, at least keeping some degree of counterforce. The second option is illustrated here. Once you are established in the chimney, and assuming it is of a nice comfortable width, your back and shoulders will be against one wall and the feet against the other. Any holds that are on the side walls of the chimney can be used for either smearing or edging and the arms can also push on the back wall of the chimney for added support. The force exerted on the opposing walls should easily be enough to keep you comfortably in position. Either technique can offer a good position for rest, allowing you to work out the moves from relative comfort.

Head requires freedom of movement to see next holds

Arms pushing against the back wall to help push up

Fingers pointing downwards allowing heel of hand to palm or push up

Back pushing against one wall

In narrower chimneys knees can be used to jam the climber in position

Knees bent to lock the climber in position

Right heel down maintaining as much friction with the rock as possible

Feet edging or smearing on the other wall

BACK AND FOOTING

This is the technique for tackling chimneys, as a means of resting and making progress. Ideally you should decide which way you are going to face before entering the chimney. It's often difficult to change your mind unless you can climb down and start again. Having made the choice, use the feet on one wall and put your back against the other. In this situation even the poorest of holds can feel good because the feet are being pushed into them, unless it is a narrow chimney. In narrow chimneys a combination of back and knee with the arm bar (see previous chapter) could be more effective, especially where there is little or nothing for the feet. There is little difference between chimneying and climbing off-widths when considering the variations of the human frame. What is a chimney for some will be an off-width for others. Use whatever holds are available for the feet.

1 The hands can be on either wall, whichever feels the most comfortable. Either way, keep the hands low, using pressure holds with the fingers pointing down and the heel of the hand on the hold.

2 To move up, push down on the back wall with your hands and bring your back off the wall. Simultaneously straighten the legs to move up and lean back as before. Now move one foot at a time and repeat the procedure.

Doing it wrong

Many people will at first find they are exerting too much pressure inside the chimney. This wastes energy that is better saved for high up the climb. Inevitably you will find yourself facing the wrong way, so be very careful in deciding what is the best option. Look where the best holds are before you start climbing; remember to look at the top of the chimney and not just for the first few moves.

◄ If you find yourself tiring quickly, it may be due to the amount of clothing you are wearing. Chimneys are fairly constricted, so you will warm up more quickly than on the face of the rock. Consider removing a layer before you start the climb.

► Remember to ease the body out just a little in order to gain height. This will reduce the resistance or drag and allow progress to be made. This is often easy to forget when you have jammed your body into the crack in order to stay in position. You have to move out to move on up, as shown here.

3 Shoulders, backside, thighs and knees can all be used to a greater or lesser extent and used in conjunction with one another for a more effective means of making progress.

4 The trick is to hold yourself in position with whatever you have and quickly move the feet. Remember to bring your body out of the crack a little as you move up. That way you're not fighting against yourself.

5 Wider chimneys will often need to be straddled, which means using one hand and one foot on either wall. This is not such a secure feeling but can be a rapid way of making progress.

Wet, wet, wet...

Practise these techniques if possible in a bouldering situation, as shown here, so you are close to the ground.

In periods of bad weather or sudden rainstorms chimneys can become natural drainage lines. They get little sun or wind and can take several days to dry out after rainfall. Even in dry conditions they can retain moisture for long periods of time, so be prepared to encounter damp, greasy rock from time to time, which can easily make them

several grades tougher than the guidebooks suggest. The chimney walls may also have been worn smooth in places by the hob-nailed boots preferred by climbers at the turn of the century.

If climbing a deep chimney, be prepared also for loose rock on ledges, because any stones dislodged will head straight for your partner. Make sure you are both wearing helmets at all times.

CORNERS

One of the most famous rock climbs in the world is known simply as "The Corner". It was first climbed in the early 1950s by the legendary Joe Brown and is a must for leaders and visiting climbers alike. A corner requires many different techniques: jamming, bridging and laybacking. We covered jamming in an earlier chapter, but climbers will need other skills to tackle climbs of this quality. Corners are like an open book with two faces and possibly a crack in the back, both to aid progress and to provide

good protection for the leader. Sometimes they can be more open, in which case they are called grooves, or more closed, in which case chimney techniques will be more appropriate.

THE PERFECT POSITION: BUILDING BRIDGES

The perfect position for tackling a corner is one where the climber can use both sides of the corner and bridge from one wall to the other, therefore utilizing holds on either wall. Use your legs to form the bridge with the feet edging or smearing on opposite walls of the corner. In some ways this is rather like the straddle across a wide chimney (see previous chapter) and works in exactly the same way. Use your hands to find holds either in the back of the corner or on either wall. This makes it possible to maintain a more upright stance and therefore a better balance.

Your head should be well away from the rock so you are able to see the next holds clearly and work out the next sequence from a resting position. Some climbers prefer to use the layback technique, but this depends on having appropriate holds and being able to push with the feet and pull with the arms in opposition. This is a much more strenuous technique but can be combined with bridging when a rest is needed.

Left hand on good "jug"

Head able to move without affecting stance to allow as much all-round visibility of the rock as possible

Arms low wherever possible to stop them tiring

Right hand using a pressure hold

Knees slightly bent to relaxed position

Right foot smearing on right wall

Body in upright stance to maintain balance

Left foot edging on left wall

Feet working in opposition

79

BRIDGING

The important point when bridging is to keep a wide field of vision because you have two or even three places to look for holds: on the left and right walls and in the corner. Because the feet are working in opposition it is not necessary to look for big footholds provided the heels are kept low. Use your weight to push the feet in position and push with the opposite hand.

Keep the fingers pointing down and use the heel of the hand on any pressure holds. Alternatively the right hand can be used to pull the right foot on while the left foot is raised. As with most climbing, keep the hands low unless using them to gain height.

Some bridging positions can be extremely wide, so there may be occasions where a leg rest is required. Do this by pushing with the right hand to rest the right leg, just as if you were going to make a move.

1 Apply additional pressure on the rock by pushing with the opposite hand. For example, apply pressure with the right hand to push the left foot on to a hold.

2 The trick now is to do the same but with the other hand and foot: the left hand pushing the right foot on, and raising the left foot.

Doing it wrong

The legs are where the main pushing power lies because the legs have the biggest muscles in the body – so use them! The most common mistake when climbing corners is to expend too much energy instead of employing good technique. Because the techniques don't feel as though they are going to work at first, you may tend to exert too much pressure, which will make you tire very quickly.

◄ If you find yourself in this position, with your feet in the back corner and hands out on the wall, you will be completely out of balance. The feet are taking too little weight and a great deal of energy is required just to maintain position. This is also likely to swing the feet away from and not on to the rock, adding to the feeling of insecurity.

Climbing corners

As with all new techniques, practise climbing corners in a bouldering situation near the ground, as shown here. It's the perfect way of honing your skills and minimizing falls and possible injuries. If climbing any higher than one or two metres (yards) off the ground, remember to wear a helmet.

Corners will often require a combination of techniques, sometimes jamming, laybacking or bridging. There will even be occasions when you might do all three different techniques in the space of three moves. Although we have now considered all the basic skills required to climb rock, it is a sport for the inventive and those who like to work all the tricky bits out for themselves.

▲ To take a rest, put both feet on one wall and your backside in the corner. This allows you to take both hands off because you are firmly wedged in position.

▲ Many corners will have a crack in the back so jamming may be an appropriate technique to gain height. Then go back to a bridging position for a rest and study the next moves.

Laybacking

This is the alternative method of climbing corners and can also be applied to crack climbing. What is required is a good edge or crack running vertically up the intended route. It is important to strike a good balance between getting the feet too high and not high enough. The former is far too strenuous because all the weight is on the arms; the latter may cause the feet to slip off. The fewer holds there are for the feet, the more you should layback.

◄ The technique is to walk the feet high until the hands and feet are in opposition. Now move the hands and feet up, taking care to move one limb at a time. It is a very effective way of making progress. The consequences of the hands or feet slipping off need only be imagined. This climber is roped as the rock face is high.

ABSEILING (RAPPELLING)

This is a technique for descending. The rope is anchored at the top, allowing a safe and controlled descent. Descending in safety is obviously of great importance. On some cliffs it is possible to scramble down an easy way, on others the easiest way down is to abseil (rappel). If you have to retreat because a climb is too hard or the weather breaks, then abseiling (rappelling) will be your only safe means of descent.

The development of modern equipment means that abseiling (rappelling) is far easier than it was, but do remember that an abseil

(rappel) is only as safe as the anchor and that cannot be truly tested until you try it for real. For many, abseiling (rappelling) has become an activity in its own right. That is fine but always remember it is dangerous and leads to many accidents and even fatalities among climbers.

THE PERFECT POSITION: GOING DOWN

The perfect position is a high anchor for easy take-off, a smooth slab where you can see all the way down and one where you can easily retrieve your ropes. This is the ideal for a beginner but as you become more experienced you're more likely to enjoy the challenge of the steeper or overhanging face. As with all rock climbing situations, the anchor must be 100 per cent secure. If it isn't, don't abseil (rappel). As in belaying, there is a live rope and a dead rope. The live rope is that below the abseil (rappel) device. Keep the feet shoulder width apart, turn slightly to the right if you're right-handed (to the left if left-handed) and watch where you're going. The difficult part is committing yourself to the abseil (rappel) but, having done that, just feed the rope out at the same speed while walking backwards down the crag. The closer you can get to the horizontal, the less likely your feet are to slip, so lean back, flex the knees and control the live rope with your lower hand. There should also be a separate safety rope or backup just in case.

Upper hand guiding the rope

Looking where going

Plenty of space between descender and backup

French prussik or safety rope as a backup

Turned towards the leading hand

Lower hand maintaining friction on the live rope and controlling the descent

Feet shoulder width apart

Feet flat against the rock for a firm stance

Knees slightly flexed, acting as shock absorbers

GETTING BACK DOWN

On a sports crag the fixed anchor point from which you will abseil (rappel) should already be absolutely secure. However, don't trust bolts implicitly, especially the older variety, and always abseil (rappel) with care. The steadier you go down, the less strain there will be on the anchor, ropes and equipment.

On traditional cliffs, life can be much more difficult and the perfect anchor is often elusive. Trees often make excellent anchors, but sadly this leads to considerable damage being caused when ropes are retrieved. However, if you absolutely have to abseil (rappel) off a tree, leave a sling in place, because this will reduce the damage. Continual abseiling (rappelling) and pulling down ropes will eventually kill the tree, resulting in even more serious damage to the crag.

Place a good anchor as high as you can. A low anchor not only increases the risk of anchor failure but makes life difficult and therefore dangerous when you're going over the edge.

Finally, choose the place where you're going to abseil (rappel) with care and make sure that no one is on their way up the cliff when you throw the ropes down. The usual climbing call to warn other climbers in your vicinity is "rope below".

▲ This high anchor point, a sling on a spike, makes life easy at the start because the anchor is above the belay device, and therefore allows the abseiler (rappeller) to achieve the correct position before going over the edge.

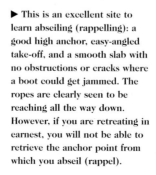

▶ This is an excellent site to learn abseiling (rappelling): a good high anchor, easy-angled take-off, and a smooth slab with no obstructions or cracks where a boot could get jammed. The ropes are clearly seen to be reaching all the way down. However, if you are retreating in earnest, you will not be able to retrieve the anchor point from which you abseil (rappel).

◀ A double rope is necessary when abseiling (rappelling) for real – retreating or descending to the bottom of the crag. If you have one rope only then find the midpoint, clip this through the anchor karabiner and throw both ends down. Feed both ropes through the abseil (rappel) device and descend. At the bottom, pull one end of the rope and the other will rise, pull through the karabiner and fall down to you. You can then create another anchor and start again.

◀ When abseiling (rappelling) for fun or to gain access to the bottom of an otherwise inaccessible cliff, you can use a single rope securely anchored at the top. You will need to take other ropes to climb with, of course. When you are back at the top of the cliff, you can easily retrieve your rope.

Going down...

The popularity of abseiling (rappelling) is partly due to most climbers' dislike of slithering down muddy paths in expensive footwear that is totally unsuited for the purpose. Abseiling (rappelling) is an essential, although inherently dangerous, technique to learn and there are many shiny gadgets available designed to make life easier. However, none are the slightest use unless the anchor point is chosen carefully with regard for the consequences. When abseiling you have to place your trust in the rope, but remember that the rope is only as secure as the anchor.

Doing it wrong

▶ A very poor site has been chosen here, especially for someone who is just learning. The rock is very steep and the lower anchor point will also make the abseil (rappel) difficult to start. The abseiler (rappeller) will be unable to see whether the ropes reach the bottom because of the extremely steep take-off point and low anchor. This will create difficulties as he goes over the edge and it is possible he will turn upside down because of the direction of pull on the anchor.

◀ This abseiler (rappeller) is too close to a climber ascending the cliff. Apart from being inconsiderate, it's proof that the abseiler (rappeller) didn't check the vicinity before he started his descent. Climbers should always take precedence over abseilers (rappellers).

ABSEIL DEVICES

The figure-of-eight abseil device is undoubtedly the best device for the job and specifically designed for the purpose, giving a controlled and safe descent. Harnesses that have a main load-bearing abseil (rappel) loop should present no problems. However, some harnesses require a karabiner to hold the leg loops up or to clip the two parts of the harness together. In some cases this will hold the karabiner in place and possibly create loading across the gate. It is important to load the rope down through the eye so that it is on top of the descender when it goes over the back bar.

Whichever device is used it is important always to use either a safety rope or a French prussik knot below the abseil (rappel) device clipped to a leg loop, as explained overleaf. This is slid down the rope by the control hand and if the hand is removed (for whatever reason) the prussik should automatically lock and stop the descent.

1 Learning or practising these skills should only take place in a controlled situation where you can concentrate on the techniques. Always use a screwgate karabiner.

2 This is a figure-of-eight descender which is loaded correctly with the rope over the connecting bar. The safety rope in this picture is attached directly to the main load-bearing loop. In this way the abseiler (rappeller) is belayed while he/she descends.

Doing it wrong

◀ In this situation a standard karabiner is being used when abseiling (rappelling). It leaves little to the imagination what the result would be if the descender flipped over and out of the karabiner. Always use a screwgate karabiner to prevent this happening.

▶ A common mistake is to allow clothing or hair to get caught in the descender. Make absolutely certain before starting a descent that all loose clothing, straps and hair are tucked away.

▶ An alternative method of providing security for the abseiler (rappeller) is to simply pull on the abseil (rappel) rope – the descender will lock and slow the descent. This helps to build up confidence in novice abseilers (rappellers) and should be used where there is no other backup. Once the first person is down, he/she can protect the rest from below by pulling gently on the rope to lock the abseil (rappel) device. This is an easy technique and requires only a little practice.

Friction

Most belay devices in common use offer reasonable options for abseiling (rappelling) and a varying degree of friction on either double or single ropes. The biggest problem with most of them is that they don't have a particularly large surface area to dissipate the heat. It is therefore important to remove the device quickly at the end of each abseil to avoid heat damage to the rope.

PERSONAL SAFETY

Although the Italian hitch is not ideal for abseiling (rappelling), it can be used in an emergency instead of a figure-of-eight descender or a belay device, although extensive twisting can occur. It is essential to use a large pear-shaped (HMS) screwgate karabiner to prevent the rope jamming and to increase the dissipation of the heat created by friction. To create an Italian hitch, form two loops, right over left and right over left, and fold the loops together. Now clip the two ropes into the karabiner. Always use a French prussik as a backup to facilitate untangling the ropes and make sure the prussik cannot be "swallowed" by the Italian hitch.

In spite of the problems this method can be used in any situation, even overhanging abseils (rappels) where the device has been dropped or forgotten. Take care to keep the French prussik short and snug. Don't use other prussik knots in this way, as they are not easily released once they have been loaded.

1 The best way of giving protection on any abseil (rappel) if you are the first to go down is to use a French prussik. This is a short loop of 6 mm (¼ in) cord wound four or five times round the abseil (rappel) rope and attached to the leg loop on the harness.

2 The loop is then slid down the rope with your lower hand as you abseil (rappel) and should lock in an emergency.

3 The crucial thing is to keep a good distance – 25 to 30 cm (10 to 12 in) – between the French prussik and the abseil (rappel) device. Use a large screwgate karabiner on the abseil (rappel) device and a smaller screwgate on the leg loop.

Keep it short

Consider also how each device will be affected if the prussik is too long. In some cases the prussik will simply be released and in other cases may be "eaten" by the device. Either way, it could be disastrous, and finding out through hard experience is not recommended. To avoid this happening, keep prussiks short and snug. There are of course some devices that are designed to lock automatically, making a French prussik unnecessary. However, a malfunction due to grit, dirt or inexperience may still occur, in which case you will look foolish if you haven't used a prussik.

TYING OFF

1 This method for locking off will work on any belay or abseil (rappel) device. Take a length of rope around the leg but keep holding the main rope.

2 Continue, taking three or four turns. This will allow any hands-off manoeuvre for either an abseiler (rappeller) or a belayer.

3 This will work equally well with all devices and allow you to sort any problems out. It must of course be practised in a safe situation near the ground – until you can do it blindfold!

Abseiling (rappelling) in safety – top tips

- Make sure your ropes reach the ground, or at least another stance.

- Get a sound anchor, at any price.

- Practise and become familiar with the technique you are using.

- Keep your anchor as high as possible in relation to where your take-off point is.

- Use a French prussik from your leg loop, and make sure it is the right length. This is usually a 1.25 metre (4 foot) length of 6 mm (¼ in) cord joined with a double fisherman's knot or an overhand knot.

- Where multiple abseils (rappels) are involved, have a sling securely attached to your harness so you can clip on to the anchor on arrival at the next stance before unclipping from the rope.

- Don't use trees unless you really have to, and then leave a sling or length of tape.

- Back the anchor up if in doubt.

- Buy yourself a mallion if your harness is a type that requires holding together at the front.

TOWARDS THE SEA

Many coastal areas boast some excellent rock climbing and offer not only superb settings for holidays, but the opportunity for some real adventure as well. Many of these areas enjoy good weather when high mountain crags are often shrouded in mist or rain, and that is one reason why sea-cliff climbing has become much more popular in recent years. There are dangers, though, and these may not be appreciated on the first few visits. A summer's evening with waves lapping gently at your feet can change radically, as anyone who has witnessed storms sweeping waves across low-lying headlands will understand. Some of these areas have tides

and offshore currents that catch the unwary and sweep them out to sea. Perhaps this is one of the attractions of climbing sea cliffs: entering a possibly hostile environment, judging the conditions and enjoying the adventure. As well as the routes that ascend the cliffs, there are also sea-level traverses, which in a calm sea can be a great pleasure to climb.

THE PERFECT SETTING: SEA AND SUN

It's a summer's day. Waves are lapping at your feet and there's just enough swell to keep you alert. Sea-level traverses are like bouldering with the extra spice of wet feet should you misjudge things. When the sea is really warm, what nicer way to finish the day than with a swim? Some traverses, however, require commitment and, should the onshore sea breezes pick up in the afternoon and bring the tide swirling in, things could change rapidly. Another perfect setting may be when the hills are shrouded in mist and the indoor wall is stuffy and laden with chalk. You feel like a breath of fresh air and the coast is bathed in warm autumnal sunshine. The routes are often steep and climbing is of the highest quality. What better than a change of scene and a great day's adventure by the sea?

PRUSSIKING

The basic techniques for climbing sea cliffs are exactly the same as for crags outdoors and for bouldering, but the different environment means that other skills and techniques must be learnt to deal with the extra hazards encountered. Many coastal areas will have only one method of approach and that's from the top, which means you will have to abseil (rappel) down before you can start your climb. There is only one way out and that is climbing. There is the possibility that you can approach at low tide, but once the tide comes in, you have to climb out or wait several hours for low tide again, by which time it could be dark.

Here is where the technique of prussiking comes in. Prussiks are short lengths of rope; the French prussik has already been described in connection with abseiling (rappelling), where it is used as a safety backup. There are many other different types of prussik knot, but in the interests of simplicity only two more are described here: the standard prussik and Klemheist prussik which are used for climbing up a rope.

STANDARD PRUSSIK

1 Take the prussik loop two or three times around the main rope and push the end through itself. Pull tight.

2 The completed knot. It is the only type of prussik knot that, with a little practice, can be tied with one hand, allowing you to hang on to the rope with the other.

KLEMHEIST PRUSSIK

1 The Klemheist prussik knot is tied with a short loop. Take the loop three or four times round the main rope and push one end through the other. Keep the joining knot of the loop out of the prussik.

2 The completed Klemheist prussik knot. It is clipped directly on to the waist harness with a screwgate karabiner. This is then slid up the rope until it can be jammed when your weight is applied.

1 Either one of the prussiks described will, with practice, allow you to make rapid progress up the rope using one loop for the foot and one tied directly to the waist.

2 Slide the foot prussik up the rope, stand on it and slide the waist prussik up too. This requires a little coordination, but this will come with practice.

3 The procedure is then repeated. Remember that when you're sitting in the harness you can take both hands off to move the other prussik, if necessary.

Problems

The main problem encountered with prussiking is keeping the prussik loops short. It would be misleading to give an exact length; climbers vary in size and you will need to find the most comfortable length for you. As a rough average, or starting length, 1.5 metres (5 feet) tied with a double fisherman's or overhand knot is about right. All prussiks should be kept "snug" on the main climbing rope, so increase or decrease the number of loops around the main rope to get the right amount of friction. It is vitally important to practise these techniques, even if you have no intention of prussiking – they may be vital to you in a particular situation. Work on the principle that if you know how to do something, you may never need the knowledge.

Don't use a French prussik on your harness as it's designed to slip and release under pressure, which is why it works so well for abseiling (rappelling).

▶ The consequence of getting it wrong, forgetting how to do it, or not knowing how to do it in the first place can only be imagined.

GLOSSARY

Abseil – A method of descending the rope using friction from a belay device or a figure-of-eight descender. The word is of German origin and often shortened to "ab". The French word rappel, "rap", is more common in the USA.

Anchor – A secure point of attachment between the climber and the rock. The attachment could be a wire, sling, nut, thread or camming device with a karabiner to which the climber attaches the rope.

Bandoleer – A rope or tape shoulder sling (often padded) to which climbing equipment can be attached and easily transferred between leader and second.

Belay – To belay: to hold the rope of the person climbing to prevent him going the full length of the rope should he fall. The belay: the location at which belaying takes place. A "good belay" denotes secure anchors for attaching the climber, a "poor belay" less so (see also Stance). On multipitch climbs the guidebook will indicate the length of each pitch, thereby indicating when to belay. Pitch 1: 15 metres (50 feet) – belay after climbing 15 metres (50 feet); Pitch 2: 33 metres (110 feet) – belay after climbing 33 metres (110 feet) etc.

Belayer – The person belaying. The "inactive" climber acts as belayer for the "active" climber.

Belay device – A friction device fitted to the rope and used by the belayer. The device allows the belayer to control the energy generated by a falling climber and arrest their fall. They are often known by trade names: ATC, Tuber, Bettabrake etc.

Below! – An exclamation used as a warning to those below you to take cover, when you knock off loose rock, or drop something.

Bolt – A fixed metal eye through which a karabiner can be clipped for protection when leading, or as a secure anchor for belaying, top-roping or abseiling. The eye is attached to a rod which is glued or hammered into a hole specially drilled in the rock.

Bouldering – A general term for climbing without ropes on small boulders or pieces of rock a few feet off the ground. Bouldering allows climbers to try difficult moves in relative safety. The activity usually involves a group of climbers trying the same moves in friendly competition.

Bridging – A method of climbing whereby the legs and arms form a bridge between the opposing walls of an open book corner. Upward progress is made by supporting body weight with one hand, moving the foot up on the same side, then repeating the process with the weight shifted on to the other hand.

Camming device – A mechanical device which can be placed in a crack for protection when leading, or as a secure anchor for belaying, top-roping or abseiling. They are often known by trade names: Friend, Camalot, Quadcam, Alien etc.

Chalk – Gymnast's chalk will improve grip when put on sweaty fingers. Chalk is carried in a small bag at the climber's back.

Clove hitch – A special knot that is easy to tie and tightens when loaded, but is easily adjusted and untied. However, it needs to be practised.

Chock – An old collective word to describe wires and roped nuts. It comes from the word chockstone, a stone or boulder jammed in a crack or gully. A chock is a piece of protection.

Descender – Better known as a figure of eight. A friction device used for abseiling.

Dynamic – A dynamic move will involve a directed lunge or jump for a hold. Climbing ropes are dynamic, absorbing the energy created by a falling climber by stretching.

Edging hold – A positive foothold on which the edge of the boot can get purchase and support, no matter how slight.

Figure-of-eight descender – See Descender.

Figure-of-eight knot – The most commonly used and strongest knot for tying a climber to a belay anchor. However, the knot is difficult to adjust and can be difficult to undo after heavy loading (see also Clove Hitch).

Guidebook – Most climbers follow established climbs in guidebooks. The guidebook will give the grade and length of the climb, describe the line it follows and where to belay. Other information may include whether the climb is strenuous, serious or relatively safe.

Harness – Specially constructed and padded waist belt and leg loops worn by the climber and into which the climbing rope is tied. Massively strong, the harness helps to absorb the energy generated in a fall.

Hold – Anything which can be used by the feet, hands or any other part of the body to aid upward progress.

Jamming - A method of climbing in which any part of the body can be securely jammed into a crack or hole in the rock to aid upward progress. The most common jamming involves the hands and feet.

Jug – A handhold that is comparatively large and so good that you feel you could hang from it all day without getting tired.

Karabiner – An aluminium alloy snaplink with a sprung gate most often used to connect the rope with protection when leading and with anchors when belaying. With screwgate and twistlock karabiners a special sleeve covers the gate to lock it closed.

Layaway – A vertical or nearly vertical hold, usually just for the fingertips. Using such holds for upward progress requires either considerable finger strength to keep the hand in place, or sufficient technique to transfer full body weight on to the hand to keep it in place.

Laybacking – A frequently strenuous and sometimes insecure method of climbing off-vertical cracks in which the hands pull down on one side of the crack and the feet push away on the other.

Leading – The process of climbing whereby the first "active" climber on the rope places protection if traditional climbing, or clips bolts if sport climbing, while the second "inactive" climber belays.

Lower-off – Most sport climbs have bolts and chains at the top from which the lead climber can be lowered by the belayer.

Mantelshelf move – A move where the feet are brought up to stand on holds being used by the hands.

Nut – A collective word to describe wires and roped nuts. A nut is a piece of protection.

Off-width – A crack that is too wide for hands and feet, but too narrow to fit the body. Climbing an off-width requires certain skills and for most people is a pretty miserable and frightening experience.

Overhand knot – A knot formed by making a loop and then drawing one end through. It is frequently used to tie off spare rope.

Pitch – Climbs that are longer than the climbing rope have to be climbed in stages. Climbers call these stages, pitches.

Piton – A metal spike with an eye which can be hammered into a crack and the eye clipped for protection when leading, or as a secure anchor for belaying, top-roping or abseiling. In the UK pitons are rarely placed when rock climbing, although many remain in place. Corrosion is a problem and they should be carefully inspected before use.

Protection – A collective name to describe a bolt, piton, wire, sling, nut, thread or camming device which the leader can clip to the climbing rope for "protection". On traditional climbs protection has to be placed by the leader and removed by the second. On sport climbs the protection is fixed in place. With traditional climbs the guidebook may indicate whether "protection" on a particular climb is good, indifferent or bad.

Prussik – A special knot used for ascending the rope. The knot jams when loaded, but can be moved up the rope when the load is released. They are usually used for self-rescue.

Quickdraw – A loop of nylon tape with a karabiner at each end, they are used for clipping the rope to protection and to facilitate easy movement of the rope through protection when climbing.

Rack – A collective name for all the protection equipment necessary for a rope of two climbers on an average climb.

Rappel – See Abseil.

Rock-over – A move involving a high step followed by a shift of body weight over on to the high leg.

Runner – Short for running belay. A running belay is the technical term for any piece of protection (wire, camming device, bolt etc) clipped to the rope by the leader.

Seconding – When the leader is securely tied to the belay anchors he can belay the second up the climb. Seconding includes belaying the leader, climbing the route second and removing the protection placed by the leader so that it can be used on the next pitch or climb.

Shake out - With exertion, lactic acid builds up, especially in the arm muscles. Hanging each arm in turn and giving it a shake helps blood flow and removal of lactic acid. Anywhere this is possible is called a shake out.

Slack – Slack rope between the climber and belayer is to be avoided as it generates greater shock loads should a fall take place, as well as increasing the distance fallen. However, slack may be needed by the second to remove protection, or by the leader when clipping overhead protection. In this case shout "Slack!".

Sling – A loop of nylon tape, usually factory sewn but sometimes hand knotted. Slings can be hung over spikes or threaded through holes in the rock and used as protection when leading, or as a secure anchor for belaying, top-roping or abseiling.

Sloper – A flat, sloping handhold that's almost impossible to get any purchase on.

Smearing – A method of using the foot to maximise friction between rubber and foothold when the hold isn't good enough to give positive edging support. You might also need to smear your hand on a sloper.

Sport climbing – Sport climbs originated in Europe and generally have fixed bolt protection. They have a different ethic and style of climbing than traditional climbs and involve a lot of falling off.

Spotting – When bouldering in pairs one climber will usually boulder while the other spots. Bouldering often involves pushing yourself to the limit close to the ground, often knowing you will fall off. Because of the short distance there is little time to "recover" before impact. A good spotter will stand close to guide your fall and prevent you stumbling and injuring yourself.

Stance – At the end of a pitch the belay may have a good stance or a poor one, regardless of how good the belay anchors are. There may be excellent anchors, but the stance is a single foothold to stand on, or the anchors may be very poor, but the stance is an excellent, roomy ledge. Most often it is something between the two.

Tape – This is another word for nylon webbing used for quickdraws, harnesses and slings. Zinc oxide tape is used by many climbers for securing sore finger tendons and for wrapping around the hands to prevent cuts when jamming.

Thread – A situation where a tape sling can be treaded through a feature in the rock and the two loops joined and used as protection when leading, or as a secure anchor for belaying, top-roping or abseiling.

Top-roping – A climbing system whereby the "active" climber is secured by a rope from above. The belayer may either be below or above the climber.

Traditional climbing – The form of climbing where protection is placed by the lead climber and removed by the second.

Traversing – Any situation where a climber moves horizontally or diagonally to the right or left for a number of moves, or even a full pitch, rather than going straight up. Unclimbable overhangs frequently have to be avoided by traversing.

Wire – Any aluminium wedge threaded on a swaged wire. In general they are too small for threading on rope or tape. They are used as protection when leading, or as a secure anchor for belaying, top-roping or abseiling. Also called nuts and chocks. Often known by their trade name: Rocks, Stoppers, RPs, Offsets etc.

ACKNOWLEDGEMENTS

The author would like to thank Perry Hawkins, Phil Creasey, Steve Hartland, Rhi Shepherd, and John and Jan Croxford for their help in realizing this book.

Thanks, too, to the experienced climbers and mountain guides who demonstrated the techniques: Libby Peter, Graham and Jackie McMahon, Gwyn Jones, Carlo Forti, Martin Crook, Nick Banks and Nigel Sheperd.

The author and publishers would like to thank the following for their generous help in providing clothing, equipment and facilities:

Plas y Brenin,
National Mountaineering Centre, Capel Curig,
Gwynedd LL24 0ET
(use of climbing wall and facilities)

Salomon Taylor Made,
Annecy House, Lodden Centre, Wade Road,
Basingstoke, Hampshire RG24 8FL
(approach shoes)

DMM,
Y Glyn, Llanberis, Caernarfon, Gwynedd LL55 4EL
(climbing hardware and rock boots)

HB Climbing Equipment,
24 Llandegai Industrial Estate, Bangor,
Gwynedd LL57 4YH
(climbing hardware and helmets)

Lowe Alpine UK,
Ann Street, Kendal, Cumbria LA9 6AB
(clothing)

Lyon Equipment,
Rise Hill Mill, Dent, Sedbergh, Cumbria LA10 5QL
(belay devices and helmets)

Troll Safety Equipment,
Spring Mill, Uppermill, Oldham, Lancashire OL3 6AA
(harnesses)

Wild Country Ltd,
Meverill Road, Tideswell, Derbyshire SK17 8PY
(belay devices)

CREDITS

INDEX